The Grail Procession

ALSO BY JUSTIN E. GRIFFIN

The Holy Grail: The Legend,
the History, the Evidence (McFarland, 2001)

The Grail Procession

*The Legend,
the Artifacts, and the
Possible Sources of the Story*

JUSTIN E. GRIFFIN

McFarland & Company, Inc., Publishers
Jefferson, North Carolina, and London

LIBRARY OF CONGRESS CATALOGUING-IN-PUBLICATION DATA

Griffin, Justin E.
    The Grail procession : the legend, the artifacts, and the
possible sources of the story / Justin E. Griffin.
        p.   cm.
    Includes bibliographical references and index.

    ISBN 0-7864-1939-3 (softcover : 50# alkaline paper)

    1. Grail—Legends—History and criticism.   2. Grail.
I. Title.
PN686.G7G748 2004
809'.9337—dc22
                               2004019456

British Library cataloguing data are available

On the cover: Joseph and companions at Wearyall Hill, at the edge of
the Glastonbury "island" painting by A.J. Davies (courtesy Neil Bonham,
St. John's Parish Church, Glastonbury); *background* ©2004 PhotoSpin

Manufactured in the United States of America

McFarland & Company, Inc., Publishers
  Box 611, Jefferson, North Carolina 28640
    www.mcfarlandpub.com

For my wife Donna, with all my love,
my thanks and, most of all, my respect.
I am very proud of you.

Also, for Mary "Granny" Patton with love.

Acknowledgments

I would like to thank all the many people who contributed to the creation of this book. First, my thanks goes to my wife, Donna, for her incredible patience and encouragement, and then to my sister Janet—both having suffered through years of listening to my theories as works in progress.

Then I would like to thank my friends with whom I have similarly shared my interests over the years. A special thank you goes to Tim Watson, who poured over the early versions of this text, making sure I didn't say anything ridiculous. Similarly deserving is John Koopmans, who not only helped me proof the manuscript, but who has always been the source of information and insights on the Grail, medieval history, and legends in general. Thanks also to Mark Fuentes, with whom I have spoken about this research for a number of years; and to Mr. Francis Thyer at Glastonbury Abbey, who has again been such a tremendous help in conducting research. Benedikt Haupt, of the Kunsthistorisches Museum in Austria, provided the rather difficult to obtain photograph of the "Spear of Destiny"; I am very grateful for his kindness and enduring patience.

Finally, a very special thank you to all the people who so generously allowed me to use the pictures and images seen in this book: Stephen Minnitt, Neill Bonham, Des Lavelle, Philippe Contal, Terry Moss, Ryoko Yoshizawa, Charles Knutson, David Freeman, Juan C. Gorostizaga, as well as Dr. Jefferson Chapman and Ms. Lindsay Kromer with the Frank H. McClung Museum on the University of Tennessee Campus. I would also like to extend a special note of thanks to the gifted artist Loreena McKinnitt. It was her song "Skellig" that first made me aware of the monastery's important role in preserving ancient manuscripts, so that they are available for us to ponder in the present day.

Contents

Preface

After completing *The Holy Grail: The Legend, the History, the Evidence,* I discovered that my course of research had left me with quite an archive of unused information about topics related to the Grail. A significant portion of this "extra" material dealt with the other relics often seen along with the Grail, which are now called the Grail Hallows: a lance, sword, and bowl. I became interested in exploring not only the history of these other relics, but why they became a lesser part of the Grail legend.

However, the study that made up the basis for this book was not simply an exercise in heating up leftovers. Far from it. It seemed like the history of these other mysterious, forgotten relics was even more obscure than that of the better known Grail. Especially intriguing for me personally was the history of the lance and how it seemed to intertwine with the history of the sword. Scholars have often misunderstood and misidentified these two relics throughout the middle ages, and I can claim the same failing. I had originally thought the lance found in Austria was not the Lance of Longinus, as was claimed, but the sword that beheaded John the Baptist. However, once I saw an image of the spear fully disassembled, it became clear that it was a simple lugged spear made to look quite different from its original appearance. It indeed looked like a Roman Gladius sword, and apparently I was not the first to have made this mistake.

In my investigation of these relics and their histories, I again encountered the theory that the Grail Hallows are reflected in the suits of the Tarot deck. This theory states that the sword, staff, pentacles, and cups seen in the modern Tarot deck were inspired by the four relics seen in the Grail procession at the castle of the Fisher King. Further, Graham Phillips made the assertion that in one very old Grail text the Tarot again makes an

1

appearance in the form of characters met along the Grail hero's path toward his goal. When I began investigating this text, I obtained a Marseilles Tarot deck and attempted to learn what secrets of the Grail legend it held. After some failed efforts, I soon saw the early Grail legend laid out before me, as well as the Biblical vision of the apocalypse and what appeared to be like a treatise on how to lead a righteous life. Seeing this, I had that wonderful feeling that, although there was no way to be sure, I was definitely on to something incredible.

The most telling, and most historically important, aspect of the Grail legend, the one thing that would go the farthest toward backing the claim that the Grail legend is based in some way on historical truth, is the "sourcebook" that Chretien claimed he was given, and which he used to create his founding version of the Grail legend. Wolfram von Eschenbach, another Grail writer, also made reference to this sourcebook, although he claimed that Chretien did not properly use this source material to tell the true story of the Grail. There are actually many references to a mysterious, cryptic text throughout Grail literature that is either closely associated with the Grail or is identified as the Grail itself. An important, almost universally accepted aspect of this sourcebook is that it tells the story of the Grail, but not to just anyone. It must be read by one who is worthy—one who knows *how* to read it. It seems our sourcebook is hidden in plain sight, still harboring its many mysteries.

This book endeavors to make sense of the myth of the Grail Hallows in light of archeological, historical and literary references to these relics (and others, commonly called the "Arma Christi"). The theory found within walks the winding path through ancient Hebraic funeral traditions, the history of early Christianity, Celtic mythology, and the foggy wastelands inhabited by history's outcasts—the Hebrew tribe of Dan, as well as the heretical sects known as the Pelagians and their later counterparts, the Cathars. Along this path lay many of history's forgotten tidbits. As a result, the path ends at what would appear to be an astounding and unexpected conclusion found among 78 images and the way in which they relate to each other.

1

The Grail Hallows

Since man first walked upon the face of the earth, he has carried with him many different types of talismans—sacred objects used for protection or reverence. Such objects have been found both in the archeological record and throughout recorded history. In fact, these simple objects, whether they be stone carvings, effigies, drawings, or writings, may be the most important part of a people's native culture. They not only can define a people, but also bind them together—or, conversely, break them apart.

These talismans, being objects of superior worth, often have ascribed to them a certain meaning or significance. One mother goddess figure might be the giver of life in the spring when the winter thaw comes, or it could be that which takes life when the seasons again turn harsh, as in the cold of winter or during droughts. However, for these objects to be sacred, they must by definition have their own particular story—a legend telling of their origins and meaning.

Since the Renaissance, the Western World has shunned such objects, relegating them to the role of antiquated ignorance that must be thrown away in order to create our modern scientific and intellectual society. However, in so doing, the proverbial baby has been thrown out with the bath water. Western ideas about legend and the mythical proclaim that modern man should eschew our long forgotten past, and instead remain focused on that which is "relevant to our time." Therefore, Western civilization fails to recognize or acknowledge the artifacts of a forgotten time that are integral parts of our common mythos.

Cultures need familiar allegories with which to define themselves. In European culture there have been no greater defining motifs than those involving the life of Christ, and that which can be called the saga of the

3

Holy Grail. While the Christian Church influenced western thought and history, the story of the Grail and other Christian relics influenced the western subconscious. The Holy Quest, as outlined in the tales of King Arthur and his knights, helped to provide a kind of order during a time of chaos and anarchy.

Although the Grail legend has become fairly popular, the full story is not as widely known. Most texts dealing with the Grail legend mention other objects—objects of equal importance that often are left out during the story's retelling. If one reads the original texts upon which the later works of writers such as Sir Thomas Mallory are based, one finds a parade of relics that pass before the heroic Grail knight's eyes. This holy spectacle is referred to as the "Grail Procession," and the relics seen therein are called the "Grail Hallows."

These Hallows, or objects of great sacredness, number four in all. They include the Holy Grail, or the cup used by Christ at the Last Supper; the spear that pierced His side as He hung crucified; the sword that beheaded John the Baptist (the son of the Virgin Mary's cousin Elizabeth, and the man who would baptize Jesus in the River Jordan); and, finally, a dish or bowl from the Last Supper. These four hallows were usually seen as part of a larger cluster of relics known as the Arma Christi, or Articles of the Crucifixion of Jesus Christ.

When depicted in paintings of the period, the Arma Christi could have included almost any Christian relic, whether it be from the Crucifixion or relics of important saints. These images could have included an assortment of heads, arms, hands, legs, feet, hearts, and other objects, as well as the more familiar items associated with the Crucifixion, such as the nails, the clothing of Christ, the shroud, the whips, a reed tipped with a sponge, and items from the Hallows (often times excluding the sword). The importance of such macabre items may be lost on modern believers, but during the Middle Ages, these were objects that pilgrims could visit, and with which they could possibly come into physical contact. To these pilgrims, relics were the mementos of their "heroes," the memorabilia of holiness. Therefore, when the Grail Hallows were introduced, it was to an audience familiar with a wide variety of holy relics.

Early Grail texts consider these items sacred in equal measure, and show them together initially, then dispersed, and finally reunited when the end of the quest is achieved. Although the manner in which these relics appear in the various stories differ, each object is in some way either overtly or archetypically present. This is how the Grail Procession is described in Chretien de Troyes' *Le Conte del Graal*.

Out of a room a squire came, clasping
a lance of purest white: while grasping
the center of the lance, the squire
walked through the hall between the fire
and two men sitting on the bed.
All saw him bear, with measured tread,
the pure white lance. From its white tip
a drop of crimson blood would drip
and run along the white shaft and
drip down upon the squire's hand,
and then another drop would flow.

Two more squires entered, and each squire
held candelabra, wrought of fine
pure gold with niello work design.
The squires with candelabra fair
were an extremely handsome pair.
At least ten lighted candles blazed
in every holder that they raised.
The squires were followed by a maiden
who bore a grail, with both hands laden.
The bearer was of noble mien,
well dressed, and lovely, and serene,
and when she entered with the grail,
the candles suddenly grew pale,
the grail cast such a brilliant light,
as stars grow dimmer in the night
when sun or moonrise makes them fade.
A maiden after her conveyed
a silver platter past the bed.
The grail, which had been borne ahead,
was made of purest, finest gold
and set with gems; a manifold
display of jewels of every kind,
the costliest that one could find
in any place on land or sea,
the rarest jewels there could be,
let not the slightest doubt be cast.
The jewels in the grail surpassed
all other gems in radiance.
They went the same way as the lance:
they passed before the lord's bedside
to another room and went inside
    [*Perceval*, Ruth Harwood Cline, pp. 87–89].

In this rendition of the procession we see only the lance and the Grail.
However, there is in this quote a short, vague reference to something else—

a silver platter that is clearly separate from the Grail. Also peculiar is that the Grail is called simply "*a* grail." Scholars believe this reference indicates the word "grail" was a common term used at the time. However, this discounts the possibility and likelihood that this simply means "one grail of several." The sword is also present, although mentioned several stanzas before this quote, and is described as being made of fine steel that will never break until a time when its bearer's life is in danger.

The passage intimates that these objects possess a certain supernatural quality—their "radiance" outshining the light from several candelabra, each of which held many candles burning brightly. Although these objects are not specifically named as Christian relics, the bleeding lance would seem to indicate a reference to the lance that pierced Christ's side at the Crucifixion.

To find the historical origins of the Grail Hallows, one must refer back to the New Testament of the Bible. Remembering that one of the Hallows is associated with John the Baptist, it is necessary to begin researching the events that took place before the ministry of Jesus. Here, at this turning point in religious history, one can see a close link between these two men—one of whom is called the last prophet of the Old Law, while the other is labeled the prophet of the New Law.

Beginning in the book of Matthew, Chapter Three, one may read about the beginning of John's ministry in the wilderness. Very soon he comes into conflict with the Roman magistrate Herod, having accused Herod of infidelity and incest. Herod has him arrested and, at the manipulative suggestion of his daughter, beheaded. This gives rise to the first of the Hallows—the sword that dispatched John the Baptist. This is the only one of the four Hallows not associated with the Passion of Christ. This may seem strange at first until one reads of the close connection between John and Jesus, beginning even before their birth. After the Virgin Mary and her cousin Elizabeth were told by an angel they would both bear sons, Mary travels to visit Elizabeth. It was said that the as-yet-unborn John leapt in his mother's womb when Mary drew near. Later, when Jesus finds John baptizing in the river, John responds that he has only cleared the way for He who is greater than himself.

The remaining three relics that comprise the Grail Hallows pertain to the life and death of Jesus. Two of these originate from the upper room in which the Last Supper was held. The Grail (in theory, the cup Jesus used at the Last Supper) and the bowl or dish were both simply food containers used during this Passover meal. The cup would have been a clay or possibly wooden vessel that either resembled or was used as a bowl. This cup also may have had a short pedestal base, depending on the wealth of the house's owner.

The dish or bowl similarly would have been made from clay or wood. If a dish, it would have been nearly flat and somewhat wider than a traditional modern dinner plate, and could also be called a platter. If a bowl, it would have been small with high sides, somewhat like a cup. Since this would have been a bowl used in the consumption of food, rather than in the serving of food, this would rule out a larger, cauldron-like bowl, as has been suggested by some medieval scholars (due to a reference in another Grail text in which the cup is said to be large enough to contain a pike or a lamprey). To some degree, the Grail and the bowl have been combined into one mythical relic; however, the earliest versions of the legend cast them as two separate objects.

The final Hallow is that of the spear, or Lance of Longinus. This is the lance that a Roman centurion used to pierce Christ's side at the Crucifixion. The typical practice was to break the legs of the crucified person to speed their asphyxiation (on the day Jesus was crucified, the Sabbath was rapidly approaching). However, this centurion made the decision to thrust a spear into His side instead. After this, it became clear that Jesus was, in fact, dead.

Learning how these items became objects of reverence requires some research. Traditional Hebrew funerary practice demanded that any objects stained by, or that held a portion of, the deceased's blood be entombed with the body. In the case of Christ's crucifixion, this would have included several sections of the cross upon which He was crucified, the nails, the spear, and any blood-stained textiles involved (such as His garments and burial cloth), as well as any blood that simply fell from the body (and which was collected in some sort of vessel). For this reason, the cup and the bowl would have been included with the body in the tomb, assuming they had once held the blood that spilled from His body. Similarly, the lance would have been entombed, assuming it could be obtained from the Roman centurion or later taken from the armory where it was kept.

Evidence indicates that the cup and bowl occupy an unusual historical position in relation to popular myth. The cup that could most readily be called the Grail was likely an agate bowl that Joseph of Arimathea purchased on his travels as a metal merchant, and intended to use for his own burial. However, this object, along with his own intended tomb, was donated for the burial of his master, Jesus. The relic most likely connected with the Last Supper is a wooden bowl found in Christ's tomb by Empress Helena in A.D. 327. This common wooden cup would have been used to collect Christ's blood at the foot of the Cross, and otherwise from the ground where it fell, while the agate cup would have been used to catch the blood from the spear wound while His body was being prepared inside the tomb. Today these cups are known by many different names and widely varied histories. The agate cup is now called the Santo Caliz de Valencia, located in Spain; and the wooden cup, the Nanteos Cup, was, until recently, held in Nanteos Manor in Wales.

As stated previously, these two cups have been combined into one by medieval scribes and poets, thus producing the modern version of the Grail legend; but in the story of the Hallows, they are separate relics. Left out of the body of popular myth, however, are the lance and the sword. It is thought that the lance was either found by Helena in the tomb along with the other artifacts previously mentioned, or that it was later recovered from the Roman armory in which it was kept (either by a group of Christians or by the centurion himself as an act of devotion).

The sword's origins are completely shrouded in mystery. Almost nothing is known about when or where it was taken after John's beheading, but it would seem from the legends and texts that it was a known and accepted relic, standing alongside the relics of Christ's Passion.

Considering the importance of blood and the objects stained by the deceased's blood in ancient Hebrew funerary traditions, why were these four objects the only relics to be included in the Grail saga? Of all the items normally depicted among the Arma Christi (which often excluded the sword of John the Baptist altogether), why did only four become the object of legend and mystery? Although it would seem logical to limit the relics included in the Grail texts to those pertaining to Christ's crucifixion, this would in itself include more objects than just four. The inclusion of the sword, a relic of John the Baptist's death instead of that of Jesus', is also quite conspicuous. What made these four specific objects somehow more special than all the rest?

One may wonder what significance these objects held in the minds and spirits of medieval Europe. It is clear that the Grail was the symbol of Christ's covenant made with mankind by drinking the wine He said was His blood, while the bowl or dish represented the commandment to eat the bread as his flesh. However, what was represented by the lance and sword? As implements of war, they would not have held the same theme of brotherhood and peace the other Hallows do. It is more likely that they reminded the earlier followers of the new Christian faith that, along with the promise of joy, there comes the reality of pain and suffering.

As time passed, the path of the Christian religion would take many turns, some leading down a rocky road filled with conflict and controversy. As the main body of the Church sought to fix the boundaries of what it meant to be a Christian, heretical groups sought to find their own answers in their own ways. This teaching of harsh reality alongside spiritual enrichment would become an important theme to one of these groups, the Cathars, who play a vital role in this investigation of the Grail Hallows and their mysteries. These four symbols would become the icons by which devotees would measure their faith, their purity, and their secrecy. Curiously, four similar symbols appear in another mystery, the collection of cards known as the Tarot, which may have had a connection to the Cathar movement. However, before one can begin to understand this era of the Hallows' history, a much earlier time period must be explored. The birth of this legend can be found where the traditions of early Christians and Celts mixed.

2

Two Paths Diverge in the Wood

What comes to mind when one hears the term *Celtic*? There are surely some standard sights and sounds that fit this description—misty green hills and meadows, mysterious stone circles and earthworks, the intricately intertwined lines in knotwork, crude implements evolving into objects of amazing beauty, and hauntingly beautiful music that speaks of great sadness. Despite the fact that most people consider all things Celtic as being "pagan" or pre–Christian, the land of the Celts possesses a Christian tradition possibly dating back to a time just after the Crucifixion. Some would even say that this was the safe harbor in which Western culture sought refuge during a stormy, troubled time.

Here is the ground on which the traditions of paganism and Christianity met and grew around each other until, in some cases, they become difficult to separate. It is not surprising that the land of the Celts is where the legend of the Holy Grail was born. In southern England, Wales, and Ireland the stories of Joseph of Arimathea, Merlin, Arthur and Perceval played out in the foggy spaces where time, history and lore become one.

One of the first discoveries made by those researching the Grail and the Grail Hallows is the very close relationship between this Christian legend and Celtic mythology. In fact, most medieval scholars would suggest that the whole legend is based entirely on Celtic mythology as presented in the Welsh *Mabinogion* and other sources. It is thought that *Le Conte del Graal* is a direct corruption of this text, rewritten only slightly to suit the Christian audience who sponsored Chretien de Troyes, the "creator" of the western Grail legend.

The Upton Country Park Romano-British Homestead. Although many homesteads commonly found during the time of Joseph of Arimathea would have been thatch roundhouses, this type of design might have been used in the building of the original wattle church, due to Joseph's exposure to Roman influence as well as the building design common to his homeland. (Photograph courtesy of David Freeman.)

Although at first glance the evidence seems clear, a deeper investigation demonstrates that the connection may not be so cut-and-dried. The story of *Peredur*, from which most of the Grail mythology is said to have been taken, was included in the *Mabinogion* when it was compiled and written in the fifteenth century. It is largely supposed that this tale is as old as the texts in the first half of the anthology, which appear to stem from an oral tradition. The fact that *Peredur* mentions the hero being part of King Arthur's court negates the possibility of an entirely pre–Christian origin.

One must then question whether the Grail itself was present before the age of King Arthur, or if the legendary king, the protagonist of many of Chretien's other works, was mixed with other myths of Celtic origin. The answer to this riddle ultimately boils down to one question: Was Joseph of Arimathea really on the isle of Britain at Glastonbury, *Insula Avalonia*,

This stained glass window depicting Joseph of Arimathea holding two cruets of Christ's blood and sweat was reassembled in the parish church of St. John the Baptist about a hundred years ago from fragments of glass painted around 1500. (Image courtesy of Neill Bonham, St. John's Parish Church, Glastonbury.)

This is an artist's rendering of what the Glastonbury of Joseph's time might have looked like. With Glastonbury Tor looming in the background as the mythical Isle of Avalon, the area surrounding modern-

shortly after the Crucifixion, as legend states? Further, did he bring to that place a vessel or vessels, identified as the Grail, later to be pursued by Arthur and his knights? Here it is necessary to seek answers from the historical records, and from the folk history of this region in southern Britain.

In reading about the life of Jesus, one discovers what are called the "lost years" of Jesus' youth. These years refer to the time between His teaching in the Temple of Jerusalem at the age of twelve, and His meeting John the Baptist in the forepart of His ministry throughout the land of Israel. While many different theories exist regarding this portion of Jesus' life, some scholars place him in the company of Joseph of Arimathea, who is said to be Jesus' uncle. It is thought that Jesus spent a great deal of this time, if not the entire period, with Joseph on his journeys as a trader of metals throughout the Mediterranean and surrounding seaboards, including the south of Britain. The following lines from the hymn entitled "Jerusalem" speak of the supposition that Jesus came to Britain with Joseph some time before the Crucifixion.

> And did those feet in ancient time
> Walk upon England's mountain green?
> And was the holy Lamb of God
> On England's pleasant pastures seen?
> And did the countenance divine
> Shine forth upon our clouded hills?
> And was Jerusalem builded here
> Among those dark satanic mills?
>
> Bring me my bow of burning gold!
> Bring me my arrows of desire!
> Bring me my spear! O clouds, unfold!
> Bring me my chariot of fire!
> I will not cease from mental fight,
> Nor shall my sword sleep in my hand,
> Till we have built Jerusalem
> In England's green and pleasant land
> ["Jerusalem," words by William Blake,
> 1757–1827].

day Glastonbury Abbey was clearly once thick marsh land. Although more recent archeological evidence indicates the Lake Village would have provided more land for each dwelling, somewhat like a private garden or grazing area, this picture suggests that the modern appearance of Glastonbury amid a peaceful, green plain once seemed much more like the misty image of Avalon. (Image courtesy of Steve Minnitt, Glastonbury Lake Village Museum, Somerset County Museums Service, U.K.)

This is the second of two images painted by A. J. Davies. This portion of the window shows Joseph and his companions arriving at Wearyall Hill at the edge of the Glastonbury "island." (Image courtesy of Neill Bonham, St. John's Parish Church, Glastonbury.)

These "Traditions of Glastonbury," as they are called, state that Joseph brought the boy Jesus to what were at the time marsh lands of Somerset to trade with the local people for tin and other metals mined from the area's landscape and waterways. They are said to have sailed there after the death of Jesus' father, and to have lived there a while, both learning from and teaching the people. It is thought that this is the reason why Joseph returned to Britain and built a church there after Christ's death. On the site of the Lady Chapel at the present day Glastonbury Abbey, Joseph erected a simple wattle church (a structure made from mud and sticks) where he kept his relics—two small cruets or vials of Christ's blood and sweat.

Since the legend of the Grail seems to have originated in Wales, near

This "Coat of Arms" was created for Joseph of Arimathea to represent the traditions of the flowering Hawthorn tree and the two cruets containing the blood and sweat of Jesus he is said to have brought to Britain. (Image courtesy of Neill Bonham, St. John's Parish Church, Glastonbury.)

Glastonbury, one may wonder if the Hallows could have been there at some point as well.

> All over Wales there are ancient roads which are called the Sarn Helen—"the causeways of Helen." Of course Helen didn't build these roads, but she is somehow connected. What seems to have happened is that Helen paraded the Cross around the country on a grand tour, before depositing it in its final resting place for safekeeping. The route that she followed then became a sort of "pilgrim's way." It is significant that you can today go along these roads following a route marked by Cross names. There is "the Pass of the Cross," "the Mountain of the Cross," "the Valley of the Cross," "the Ford of the Cross," "the Vale of the Cross," "the Fields of the Cross" and so on [*The Holy Kingdom*, Gilbert, Wilson, Blackett, p. 141].

Despite this story about Empress Helena, the mother of Constantine the Great, parading the relics found in Christ's tomb around the Welsh countryside, no evidence exists—nor does any folklore claim—that the spear or sword ever came to Britain. Even the Santo Caliz, the Grail cup that likely inspired the popular vision of the legend, only traveled through Rome and Spain. Tradition states that the Grail legend in Britain originated with Joseph's two vials; while evidence suggests that they were merely two of several, all of which contained a small portion of Christ's blood, poured from the Santo Caliz into these smaller flasks.

However, the only known direct historical reference to the Grail, made by the fifth-century Greek historian Olympiodorus, suggests that another Grail, called the "Marian Chalice," was found in the tomb and later sent to Britain in A.D. 410 for safety during the barbarian invasion of Rome. Since the Santo Caliz never reached Britain, another possible source of the Grail legend is the Nanteos Cup, which was allegedly found hidden in the walls of Glastonbury Abbey and later taken to the monastery of Strata Florida near Nanteos for safe keeping during the dissolution of the monasteries throughout Britain.

The arrival of the cup at Glastonbury no doubt refueled the Grail tradition at the abbey, but it is unclear how the lance and the sword entered the picture. The only known history of the lance places it in Jerusalem, after which time it gets bounced around Eastern Europe and the Middle East, until it finally comes to rest at the Vatican in Rome.

Much less is known about the sword and John the Baptist. The sword's place in history might have been lost completely if not for a peculiar relic housed at the Hoffburg Museum in Austria. Although relics of St. John the Baptist can be found throughout the Old World (including pieces of his skull, and various fingers and limbs), one story of his grave being found beneath a Coptic monastery sheds some light on the fate of his relics.

The Hebrew historian Josephus gives us perhaps the best and clearest account of historical events that took place around the time of John and Jesus. It is, in fact, Josephus' record, as much as the archeological record, against which the history of Biblical events is measured. The following passage retells his version of the John story.

> When and where the Precursor met Herod, we are not told, but from the synoptic Gospels we learn that John dared to rebuke the tetrarch for his evil deeds, especially his public adultery. Herod, swayed by Herodias, did not allow the unwelcome reprover to go unpunished: he "sent and apprehended John and bound him in prison." Josephus tells us quite another story, containing perhaps also an element of truth. "As great crowds clustered around John, Herod became afraid lest the Baptist should abuse his moral authority over them to incite them to rebellion, as they would do anything at his bidding; therefore he thought it wiser, so as to prevent possible happenings, to take away the dangerous preacher...and he imprisoned him in the fortress of Machaerus" (Antiq., XVIII, v, 2) [*The Catholic Encyclopedia: Saint John the Baptist*].

Of particular interest in this passage is the name of John's prison—Machaerus. In an Egyptian Coptic monastery of the same name, monks discovered a vaulted tomb under a chapel dedicated to John the Baptist. Although legends told of the remains of the prophet called "the Precursor" being hidden at this monastery, no one ever put much credence in the story until one monk, placed in charge of a monastery renovation, noticed something strange in the chapel's location. Chapels consecrated to John the Baptist are usually placed to the south of the main sanctuary in most Coptic monasteries. However, the chapel of St. John in this monastery is located to the north.

In addition to this strange exception to the normally stringent rules, there is a tradition of burning incense at the base of one particular pillar inside the northern chapel on the feast of John the Baptist—a tradition dating back to the beginning of the order at Machaerus. Excavation at the spot revealed a wooden coffin containing the eighteenth century remains of one of the church's patriarchs. However, something even more intriguing was found under this coffin—a narrow vertical passage leading to a vaulted chamber partially filled with dirt. Sifting around in the loose soil reportedly revealed a human skull, quickly followed by an entire skeleton. The traditions of John the Baptist at the monastery of Machaerus led the monks to believe that this was the final resting place of the Precursor, as

John has been called, and that the remains found there were of the man himself. Although it would appear that no other relics were found, this discovery suggests that his relics had been scattered abroad and later hidden, much as the relics of Christ's Passion were scattered in legend.

The story of the Hallows as told above is referred to as the "Christian Branch" of the story. Some medievalists argue that the true cycle of the Hallows began much earlier in Celtic myth. Despite some evidence to the contrary, this theory initially seems valid, as there appears to be a close relation between Celtic mythology and the objects that make up the Hallows of Christian legend. The Grail cup, dish, lance, and sword seem to be based on the Celtic Cauldron of Dagda, the Lia Faill (or Stone of Destiny), the Spear of Lugh, and the Sword of Nuada (or the Sword of Rhydderch).

> The echtrai, or adventures from which the Grail romances were originally drawn, tell of fantastic visitations of heroes to the island realms and palaces of gods and immortals. Here valorous warriors are sumptuously entertained with food and drink, magically served by golden Vessels of Abundance. In these Celtic other-worldly elysiums neither the inhabitants nor the visitors appear to age. Mystical talismans, magical chessboards, enchanted swords and supernatural spears all bestow their various powers and plenitude. We will shortly be introduced to such artifacts as a Drinking Horn of Plenty, or a Cauldron of Rebirth and Knowledge, which find their counterparts within the later Grail legends. [The Holy Grail: Its Origins, Secrets, & Meanings Revealed, Godwin, p. 17].

It is supposed, upon reading tales such as Peredur from the Welsh Mabinogion, that medieval writers such as Chretien de Troyes simply utilized these pagan Celtic stories and reworked them to reflect the values and tastes of their medieval Christian audiences. It is easy to see how such an assumption arose, since there is an uncanny correlation between the Grail legend and these Celtic works, most noticeably between the Welsh Peredur and Chretien's Conte del Graal. In later continuations of the French work, for instance, one of Joseph of Arimathea's followers is named Bron—very similar to Bran the Blessed from Celtic mythology. The head contained in the bowl identified with the Grail in Peredur is assumed to be that of this Celtic figure.

The classical Grail figure of the Fisher King or King Fisherman is also clearly identified with Celtic tradition. According to legend, the Fisher King, often considered to be Bran, is said to have been wounded in the thigh or the "loins" by a lance or javelin, causing him to become suspended between life and death, and his realm to become a land suspended between prosperity and doom. This concept of the king of the realm being supernaturally tied to the fate of his land is not only a Celtic tradition, but also one that dates back to the beginning of kingship. Thus the Grail cup is seen as a cauldron of rebirth in that the Grail must be obtained by the Grail hero in order to "heal" the wounded spirit and body of the Fisher King, allowing him to pass on into the Otherworld, and so restore his kingdom to its former state of plenty.

Although the legends of Bran the Blessed and the Fisher King paint a very Celtic picture of the Hallows, historians and scholars of medieval literature credit the creation of the Hallows to the Celtic tradition of the Tuatha de Danaan, or Faery Folk. Little is known about these people historically. They have come down through history mostly in the form of legend. Said to be "shining faced," tall, and fair-skinned, the Tuatha are claimed to have been highly intelligent people from the lands to the north. Their mythical origins as "supernatural beings" or "fairies" coming to Britain out of the mist probably originated from their practice of burning their boats upon reaching the Scottish shore so that they could not return to their land of origin.

This tradition claims that they passed through the lands of Scotland and eventually came to Ireland, where they defeated its native population, creatures known as Firbolgs. The owners of these Celtic Hallows were members of the original Tuatha. Dagda, the leader of the Tuatha, is called the "Good god," and is said to have both superhuman strength and appetite, possessing the cauldron of neverending nourishment. The Lia Faill, although not associated with any particular god, is still revered today as the Stone of Scone, the Stone of Destiny, and the stone on which Jacob laid his head when he dreamed of his stairway leading to Heaven. Lugh, a craftsman and possessor of a magical spear, is said to have led the Tuatha to victory at the battle of Mag Tuireadh, and is still celebrated today at the August 1st festival of Lugnasad. Finally, Nuada, holder of the magical sword, is known as "Nuada the Silver-Handed" because he lost his hand, and thus the leadership of the Tuatha, at the Battle of Mag Tuireadh.

The Tuatha de Danaan have been called alternately "The Children of the Goddess Danu," "People of the earth mother Anu," and descendants of the lost Hebrew Tribe of Dan. Their magical weapons and relics that seem to correspond to the four Grail Hallows are actually a part of the larger 12 Treasures of Britain—a list of objects reappearing in Celtic folklore. Although the stories of the Fisher King and the Tuatha de Danaan appear to indicate a Celtic origin for the legends and mysteries found in the tales of the Grail and its Hallows, historical references outside the body of this mythology indicate otherwise. However, these similarities and references should not be taken lightly. In fact, these tales of mythical relics and mysterious people may in fact lend themselves to the theory that these Christian Hallows were not only real, but also present in the land of the Celts, making a noticeable impact on their culture. However, to understand this paradoxical theory, one must understand the basics of Celtic culture and mythology. Only with that understanding will the mysterious Fisher King and the Tuatha de Danaan leave the realm of myth and enter the land of history.

3

Firbolgs, Danus, and Dragons on the Water

Mythology and history make strange bedfellows. Anyone investigating mythology invariably encounters two opposing camps. On one side stand those who feel mythology should be left to the dark recesses of the long-ago human mind. On the other side are those who acknowledge the validity of knowing and understanding mythology, but who question the necessity of learning what inspired such legends. In a sense, mythology defines a culture as much as its geography, technology, or belief system. Regardless of where a culture stands today, mythology tells where it stood a thousand yesterdays ago.

A good example of this from western culture is the concept of a flat earth. The medieval mind saw the world as flat, like the ground on which man walked, with a very definite edge—the peril being that if one ventured too far into the distance, into the unknown, one risked falling off the world into the abyss. Since even the dangers remained unknown, the maps of the time simply described these dangerous areas by stating, "HERE THERE BE DRAGONS." Now that this myth has been dispelled, the western world defines itself as a culture of exploration and discovery; yet the phrase "to the ends of the earth" remains in common usage.

To investigate the legend of the Hallows is truly to immerse oneself in an investigation of Celtic myth. Since most texts seeking to find a source for the legends of the Grail and the Hallows assume a Celtic origin, it is necessary to see what Celtic mythology really says about these enigmatic relics. To do so is to descend into a realm of warfare, surreal darkness and honored heroes who surpassed both. In Celtic myth, the King Arthur with which we are so familiar journeys to the dark land of the Underworld in search of magical objects. The Grail is seen as one such magical object, born in the nighttime fires of Celtic religions but now changed to the cup of the Christian Eucharist. One may wonder where myth ends and history begins, not to mention how to tell them apart. The task is to learn as much as possible of both history and myth, and find where they intersect. It is there where the historical reconstruction of myth can begin.

The pantheon of Celtic gods appears like that of most other pre–Christian religions. Included are gods of war, the sun, the moon, the harvest (plenty), life, death, and rebirth. These gods and their traditions reflected what was pertinent to the Celts at this time. The gods of Dagda, Anu, Lugh, and Nuada have already been introduced, but possibly the most famous among these is Bron, or Bran the Blessed.

The god of sun, animals, poetry and music, Bran the Blessed is said to have journeyed in the Underworld for many years, doomed to death upon his return to Ireland. After his death, his head was buried in what is now London (in order to ward off invasion). Below are selected excerpts from *The Voyage of Bran*, with stanzas pertaining to songs sung during the course of the story removed.

> 32. Then on the morrow Bran went upon the sea. The number of his men was three companies of nine. One of his foster-brothers and mates was set over each of the three companies of nine. When he had been at sea two days and two nights, he saw a man in a chariot coming towards him over the sea. That man also sang thirty other quatrains to him, and made himself known to him, and said that he was Manannan the son of Ler, and said that it was upon him to go to Ireland after long ages, and that a son would be born to him, even Mongan son of Fiachna, that was the name which would be upon him.

> 61. Thereupon Bran went from him. And he saw an island. He rows round about it, and a large host was gaping and laughing. They were all looking at Bran and his people, but would not stay to converse with them. They continued to give forth gusts of laughter at them. Bran sent one of his people on the island. He ranged himself with the others, and was gaping at them like the other men of the island. He kept rowing round about the island. Whenever his man came past Bran, his comrades would address him. But he would not converse with them, but would only look at them and gape at them. The name of this island is the Island of Joy. Thereupon they left him there.

> 62. It was not long thereafter when they reached the Land of Women. They saw the leader of the women at the port. Said the chief of the women: 'Come hither on and, O Bran son of Febal! Welcome is thy advent!' Bran did not venture to go on shore. The woman throws a ball of thread to Bran straight over his face. Bran put his hand on the

ball, which clave to his palm. The thread of the ball was in the woman's hand, and she pulled the coracle towards the port. Thereupon they went into a large house, in which was a bed for every couple, even thrice nine beds. The food that was put on every dish vanished not from them. It seemed a year to them that they were there, it chanced to be many years. No savour was wanting to them.

63. Home-sickness seized one of them, even Nechtan the son of Collbran. His kindred kept praying Bran that he should go to Ireland with him. The woman said to them their going would make them rue. However, they went, and the woman said that none of them should touch the land, and that they should visit and take with them the man whom they had left in the Island of Joy.

64. Then they went until they arrived at a gathering at Srub Brain. The men asked of them who it was come over the sea. Said Bran: "I am Bran the son of Febal," saith he. However, the other saith: "We do not know such a one, though the Voyage of Bran is in our ancient stories."

65. The man leaps from them out of the coracle. As soon as he touched the earth of Ireland, forthwith he was a heap of ashes, as though he had been in the earth for many hundred years.

66. Thereupon, to the people of the gathering Bran told all his wanderings from the beginning until that time. And he wrote these quatrains in Ogam, and then bade them farewell. And from that hour his wanderings are not known [*The Voyage of Bran*].

This quintessentially Celtic tale speaks of a man who sets out upon the sea, being cursed if he ever returns home, and arrives in the Celtic Underworld, Avalon—a land of joy in the absence of want. In many ways, this describes the legendary journey of Joseph of Arimathea to Britain. He set out upon the sea, and traveled to the distant land of Britain, most likely knowing he could never return to his native Israel. When he arrived at Britain, he settled at Glastonbury, which has been called Avalon, with his company and family.

This similarity becomes all the more pronounced when one reads in the Bran text, only a few stanzas before the above excerpt, how a magical branch passes from a woman's hand to Bran's and back again. The classical retelling of the Joseph of Arimathea legend states that when Joseph and company came within sight of the present grounds of Glastonbury atop Wearyall Hill, Joseph struck the ground with his staff, causing it to erupt in flowering leaf and bloom. While this may seem like yet another example of the Christianized story with which we are familiar being taken from Celtic tradition, the *Voyage of Bran* text dates from the seventh or eighth century A.D.—some 600 to 700 years after Joseph's time.

Apart from the obvious links between Bran or Bron and Joseph of Arimathea, the possible Celtic origin of the Hallows legend stems from the previously mentioned Tuatha de Danaan, the "parent deities" of the Celts. These mythical people are the possessors of magical vessels, spears, swords, and other objects that sound very much like the traditional Grail Hallows. Therefore, to determine if they were in fact the inspiration for the objects of Christian veneration as described in legend, one must know a little more about them in order to make a final judgment.

The Tuatha de Danaan, or Children of Danu, are seen as "Faery Folk" in Irish mythology, inhabiting their fairyland realm of Tir-Na-Nog (quite different than the portrayal painted by historians such as Herodotus and the Venerable Bede). The story of the Tuatha begins not in the land of Mother Goose, but the motherland of western civilization, Greece.

According to references scattered throughout the history of the ancient world, these Celtic deities originated as a nomadic, ocean-going people who eventually came into conflict with the Greeks. Initially called Pelasgians, this loose-knit band would ultimately disperse, disappearing into other cultures around the Mediterranean. Some, however, are said to have strayed to the North where they became the founders of the Danish people. Denmark, say proponents of this theory, is derived from the term "Daanmark," or the "Land of the Daans."

According to the legend of the Tuatha, they arrived on the Scottish shores, emerging from a cloud of mist. Despite the fanciful accounts of their supernatural origins, this mist was not the mists of legend but the smoke rising from their own burning boats. The items that have been associated with the Hallows were brought with them from their greatest cities—the cauldron of plenty was brought from Murias, the Stone of Destiny came from Falias, the lance was carried from Finias, and the sword taken from Gorias.

After some time, they moved to the island now known as Ireland, where they drove out the native Irish people, whom they called the Firbolgs. Here they ruled in peace for several hundred years. However, as any student of European history knows, peace in that part of the world is short-lived. A race of people arrived on their coasts that the Tuatha found invincible in battle. Eventually these people, known as Picts, were persuaded to claim the lands to the north of those settled by the Tuatha. The final invasion—and defeat—came to the mythical Tuatha at the hands of the Milesians. According to legend, the Tuatha de Danaan met defeat in a series of battles that lasted one year. During these battles, the great kings of the Tuatha fell, leaving behind only their queens. It is said the old name for Ireland, "Eire," is in honor of their Queen Eire.

It is from this point that the history of the Tuatha de Danaan enters the realm of myth. After their defeat by the Milesians, they retreated to the great earthwork at Tara, where they joined with the immortal Sidhe—the spirits of wood and stone. After many years in this paradise realm, the now-otherworldly Tuatha de Danaan left the mound at Tara and returned to the mists of Tir-Na-Nog.

The reference to the Picts confronting the Tuatha now brings accepted European history to the forefront of this discussion. During the Dark Ages, Britain was flooded by invasions from several different peoples, such as the Jutes, Picts, and Irish. However, none of these cultures made as deep and long-lasting an impact as the Anglo-Saxons.

These Anglo-Saxon "invaders" were not invaders in the strictest sense. In fact, they were hired by Prince Vortigern as mercenaries during the fifth-century power struggles that typified Dark-Age Britain. After this uneasy alliance went sour, the Anglo-Saxons seized lands throughout southern England for settlement. Coming from Holland, Denmark and Western Germany, they brought with them their own form of runic writing, and a rich body of oral tradition—which included histories and legendary sagas.

Much of what today is considered inherently "Celtic" is derived from these cultures—their influence clearly visible in the region's art, folklore, and archeology. Therefore, one may wonder what influence it had on the legend of the Grail Hallows. In many texts dealing with these enigmatic relics, the Anglo-Saxon fingerprint can clearly be seen.

While the decorations found in most early Celtic settlements reflect a heavy interest in spiral patterns and other simple forms, one of the best examples of Celtic Irish artistry, the *Book of Kells*, possesses its own very distinct flavor, demonstrating a very pronounced Anglo-Saxon style. It accurately depicts human forms, as well as elaborately stylized images of animals, both real and fantastic. Even many of the illuminated letters throughout the book have a runic appearance.

When one compares examples of Viking and Danish artwork to that of this time period in the British Isles, a very striking similarity becomes apparent. While the *Book of Kells* still exhibits the typical Celtic spirals and geometrical patterns, the degree of complexity is far greater than the simple tribal art found in many early Celtic settlements. A noticeable example of this Celtic/Nordic similarity is seen in the animal figures in the *Book of Kells*. While Celtic depictions of animals are often anthropomorphic, indicating the Shamanistic tradition, many animals in the book of Kells have features—such as raised claws, bulging eyes, and bared teeth—reminiscent of the Viking tradition (as seen in the symbolic heads on the fore and aft posts of their longboats).

While the artwork of this period reflects an Anglo-Saxon influence, another fingerprint can be found in many of the stories about the Grail

These two images illustrate the type of spiral patterns and other designs found in many ancient structures scattered around the British Isles and other parts of Europe. These specific examples are found at the passage tomb called Newgrange in Ireland. Although images such as those found in the *Book of Kells* are considered to be typical "Celtic" motifs, these images demonstrate that artwork in Britain looked quite different before the arrival of the Anglo-Saxons. (Photographs courtesy of Ryoko Yoshizawa.)

and its Hallows. A board game called gwyddbwyll (much like modern chess) is described in such Arthurian texts, both in the *Mabinogion* and in the tales of Chretien de Troyes. A king (most often associated with the Fisher King in his Grail Castle) is seen playing this game with a page or a maiden on a silver board lined with golden pieces. Although the specific characteristics of this game vary, it is most often likened to the Anglo-Saxon game called *towlbwrdd*, or tablut, in which the layout of the pieces suggests a much more fierce situation than that seen on a chess board.

In tablut, the pieces consist of the king (which is placed in the center of a nine-by-nine board), the princes (two of which protect the king at each of the four cardinal directions), and 16 enemies (representing members in four opposing armies) arranged in a triangular pattern, pointing to the lines of princes defending the king. The objective of tablut is to use

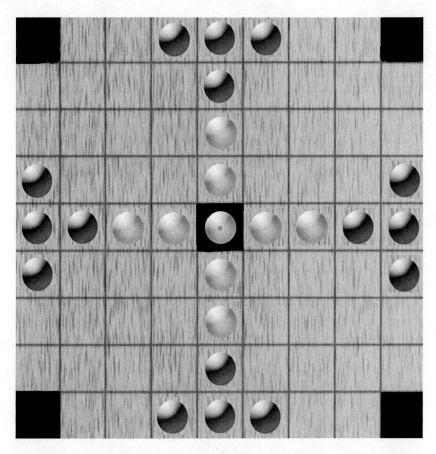

The medieval Anglo-Saxon game of Tablut. A distant ancestor of our modern chess, it shows a scenario of a trapped king assaulted on all sides by opposing forces. The deceptively simple goal: reach the safety of one of the four corner squares.

the princes to push back the opposing armies and forge a clear path through which the king can escape to one of the four corners of the board, with each piece only allowed to move vertically or horizontally, never diagonally.

This game paints a picture of a king and kingdom attacked on all sides, the king making his way to safety in what one would assume is a neighboring, friendly kingdom. Although the odds against the king seem staggering, the game itself is rather simple to win. If the princes immediately move as a wall to block the enemy pieces, the king will have a clear path, untouchable by the opposing pieces, to safety at any corner.

It is interesting to note that, in contrast to the quiet, sedate game of chess (in which two neat lines of forces require nested layers of strategy for victory), tablut suggests a much more vicious struggle among several warring factions, and yet makes it quite simple for the king to prevail. To make the matter of tablut/gwyddbwyll more peculiar, the game sometimes takes on magical connotations, with the pieces moving themselves around the board, much in the same manner as witnessing a mystical vision of things to come. In his book *The Holy Grail : Its Origins, Secrets, & Meaning Revealed*, Malcolm Godwin describes another version of the game in which the cards of the Tarot deck are used as playing pieces, imbuing the manner in which the game plays out with its own particular meanings.

One may therefore wonder if this game of a surrounded king slipping away from his captors may have some special meaning in the context of the Grail tradition. The inclusion of a simple board game into a Grail text may not seem conspicuous at first; however, its appearance in nearly all early Grail texts indicates that its presence carries some meaning. Although it remains unlikely that this meaning will ever fully be understood, it does introduce the notion that simple items, even games, can provide important historical allusions and other information relevant to the modern researcher.

Although typically it has been thought that the Anglo-Saxon invaders violently overtook the native peoples they encountered, it has been suggested that, at least in some cases, these people accepted their "Anglicanization," choosing to embrace the Anglo-Saxon way of life rather than having it forced upon them. This may explain the close association with things Anglo-Saxon and that which is customarily called Celtic in modern western society.

In any event, the influence of the Anglo-Saxons on the British Isles during the Dark Ages was as powerful, and is still as tangible, as the dramatic influence made on the entire world during the British Colonial period of modern history. Therefore, one may legitimately wonder how this culture influenced the traditions that shaped the legend of the Hallows. Would it have been possible for these Nordic people to somehow associate four Judeo-Christian relics with four magical objects belonging to the Faery Folk—the Tuatha de Danaan? The answer to this question can be found in a land even more distant from Britain than the realm of the Vikings. To fully understand the tradition of the Danaan requires one to learn more about the land of Israel—the home of Jesus and of the mysterious 12 Tribes.

4

The Tribe of Dan

From an archeological standpoint, there can be no more mysterious or involving a subject to study than the Bible. Stories in the Bible have led archeologists to forgotten peoples and ancient cities, such as Jericho, Ubar, and the golden tombs and bull lyres of Ur. Until the age of the antiquarian, the Bible was accepted as the most trusted record of prehistory, and was once used to calculate the age of the earth using Jesus' genealogical history. Obviously, the Bible is important when researching the historical aspects of the Grail and the Hallows; but one factor comes not out of the New Testament, but the Old Testament. In fact, the earliest stories from the Bible give rise to yet another legend that greatly impacts this investigation of the Hallows.

The history of the Hebrew people is a continuing story of humble beginnings giving rise to greatness, pride and overconfidence, and finally subjugation by another culture. However, despite their captivity, these people flourished and grew, invariably increasing in power and influence until they were again in a position of greatness as God's "chosen people." This scenario played itself out over and over in the Bible, producing such well known stories as Moses leading his people out of Egyptian bondage, and the downfall of the Kings of Israel. Of these examples, it is the latter that provides a possible link to the origins of the Celtic Hallows, or Treasures of Britain, and their association with the Tuatha de Danaan.

Jerusalem was formally established when King David, a great warrior and leader of the Jewish people, brought the Ark of the Covenant to Mount Moriah. His intent was to build there a great temple to God, and make it the center for the worship of their god, Yahweh. However, because David was a man who lived by the sword, God told him he could not build His

31

temple. This task would fall to his son, Solomon. While the Temple was being built, the Ark sat under a vast tabernacle, called the "Tabernacle in the Wilderness," that served as a temporary temple until the vast Temple of Solomon could be finished. When the towering shrine of gold and jewels was completed, the Ark was moved into the inner sanctum, then called "the Holy of the Holies," where it remained until it was lost to history. Solomon was renowned for his wisdom and fairness, and his kingdom stood at the pinnacle of the golden age of kings.

However, this golden age was not to last. Solomon's close ties to, and acceptance of, other cultures slowly led to an abandonment of the Hebrew God and practices. Solomon's desire for opulence and riches led to the oppression of his own people, and eventually to his own downfall. In the years following the end of his rule, the nation of Israel divided into twelve tribes that became further separated into two "houses"—the southern kingdom, or House of Israel (which became the modern Jewish people), and the northern kingdom, called the House of Judah. It was the ten tribes of the House of Judah that became the "Lost Tribes of Israel," who allegedly scattered and continued to travel across what is now Europe.

This assertion comes largely from verses in the Old Testament, such as that in Genesis 28:14, which reads:

> And thy seed shall be as the dust of the earth, and thou shalt spread abroad to the west, and to the east, and to the north, and to the south, and in thee and in thy seed shall all the families of the earth be blessed.

This, claim the proponents of the theory, describes what became of the "lost tribes" of Israel. Simply put, they spread out across the lands of the earth, mostly in Europe, becoming part of the native people they found there, and influencing their cultures.

Among these world travelers was the Tribe of Dan, who for a time lived among the Greeks, and would later become the Tuatha de Danaan. Yair Davidy, a researcher of the lost tribes of Israel, asserts that the god who founded Greek culture, Danaus, could in fact be associated with the Danus, or Tribe of Dan. These Israeli nomads who became part of the Greeks and later the Irish have been called by many names throughout history: the Hyksos, the Danaioi, the Pelasgians, the Tuatha de Danaan, and the Cymri. Of these names, the Tuatha is already familiar; however, two more will prove quite important as well—Pelasgians, and Cymri.

Most students of British history are familiar with the legend that Britain was founded by the Roman hero Brutus who lends his name to the island nations. Supporting this idea of a British Mediterranean heritage is the Welsh name for Wales, "Cymru"—quite similar to the name given to the Tribe of Dan, "Cymri." However, one need not rely merely on this similarity to put credence in the idea of a Hebrew Tuatha. The following is taken from the writings of Homer regarding the Danites.

> Danaus, the father of fifty daughters, on coming to Argos took up his abode in the city of Inarchos and throughout Hellas. He laid down the law that all people hitherto named Pelasgians were to be named Danaans.

Homer further cements the association with the following passage.

> They say that those who set forth with Danaus, likewise from Egypt, settled what is practically the oldest city of Greece, Argos, and that the nations of the Colchi in Pontus and that of the Jews, which lies between Arabia and Syria, were founded as colonies by certain emigrants from their country.

It is clear from these quotes that the Danaans and the Pelasgians (both names referring to the Tribe of Dan) were one in the same.

A link to the Old Testament can also be found in one of the Hallows itself. The Lia Faill, the stone from the island of Faill to the north of the Britannic Isles, is also called the Stone of Scone, or the Stone of Destiny.

> And he lighted upon a certain place, and tarried there all night, because the sun was set; and he took of the stones of that place, and put them for his pillows, and lay down in that place to sleep.
> And he dreamed, and behold a ladder set up on the earth, and the top of it reached to heaven; and behold the angels of God ascending and descending on it.
> And behold, the LORD stood above it, and said, I am the LORD God of Abraham thy father and the God of Isaac: the land whereon thou liest, to thee will I give it, and to thy seed [The Holy Bible, KJV, Genesis 28:11–13].

According to legend, this is the stone upon which Jacob slept when he dreamt of Heaven, and upon which every great king of the British Isles has been crowned. This, more than any other evidence previously cited, demonstrates the strange mingling of Celtic legend, Nordic traditions, and the stories of the Old Testament. A researcher of the Hallows legend may find this to be a strange mixture; however, as is the case with most legends, the places where the most contrasting threads intersect are often the places where legend, history, and reason come together.

Investigating the history behind the legend of the Lost Tribes of Israel is a complex process, one involving tales steeped in mystery which are to some, hard to believe at best. But it is not necessary to believe the Lost Tribes theory to realize its relevance to a discussion of the Hallows. All one needs to believe is that the people of the time possessed this belief—that a legacy of descent from the Tribes of Israel existed throughout Dark-Age Europe. Not only did the legend of the Tribes influence culture during this time, it propagated itself through history as legend, taking the form of the Cymri and Pelasgians, and finally the Tuatha de Danaan. This belief is seen quite clearly in the Scottish Declaration of Independence, which specifically claims that the Scottish people are descended from the Tribes of Israel.

> Most Holy Father and Lord, we know and from the chronicles and books of the ancients we find that among other famous nations our own, the Scots, has been graced with widespread renown. They journeyed from Greater Scythia by way of the Tyrrhenian Sea and the Pillars of Hercules, and dwelt for a long course of time in Spain among the most savage tribes, but nowhere could they be subdued by any race, however barbarous. Thence they came, twelve hundred years after the people of Israel crossed the Red Sea, to their home in the west where they still live today. The Britons they first drove out, the Picts they utterly destroyed, and, even though very often assailed by the Norwegians, the Danes and the English, they took possession of that home with many victories and untold efforts; and, as the historians of old time bear witness, they have held it free of all bondage ever since. In their kingdom there have reigned one hundred and thirteen kings of their own royal stock, the line unbroken by a single foreigner [*The Declaration of Arbroath*].

Regardless of one's personal views on the topic of the Tribes of Israel, the study of the Hallows finds in Denmark the one place where the legends of the Lost Tribes, the Tuatha, and the Hallows come into historical contact. According to the history of the Lost Tribe of Dan, some time after these traveling Hebrews left Greece, they arrived in the northern lands now known as Denmark.

Thomas Moore agrees with this in the *History of Ireland* (volume 1, p. 59), stating that the Firbolgs of Ireland were overrun by the Tuatha after they fled Greece, and settled for some time in Denmark and Norway. This is the point at which the Tribes of Israel become relevant to the Hallows (or, more correctly, four of the Treasures of Britain). The legend of the magical items originating from the lands to the north, coming to Britain in the hands of the Tuatha de Danaan, finds it roots in the tradition of the Tribe of Dan, known and perpetuated by the Anglo-Saxon invaders coming to the British Isles.

History does not readily accept the notion of change. That is, when an idea becomes accepted as "history," it becomes a concept difficult to change. In that sense, if one does not accept the theory that the Tribes of Israel founded Denmark or Ireland, it becomes all the more difficult to accept the idea that a culture such as the Celts, who are incorrectly considered by many to be "indigenous," might have traditions that were influenced by other cultures. That is to say, if these people were indigenous, what culture could have influenced them?

Consider the theory that the first Christian church in Britain was founded by Joseph of Arimathea and his followers only a few years after the death of Jesus around A.D. 33. With respect to the long-standing Celtic tradition in Britain, this event occurred relatively close to the arrival of the Celtic people around 200 B.C. Perhaps the arrival of these people from the distant shores of Palestine mirrored the tale of the coming of the Tuatha de Danaan to Britain. One might even envision Joseph of Arimathea and his small band of followers burning their boats on the British shores, knowing that as outcasts they could never return to their native homeland. Although this idea is intriguing, it is most likely that the tradition of the Tuatha de Danaan in Celtic mythology had much to do with the Anglo-Saxon invasions around A.D. 500. How is this possible? Once again, the originating legends of the Tribe of Dan provides the necessary link.

The key to this association comes from the stories of the Tuatha journeying from lands to the North. If the legends of Joseph at Glastonbury are true, that places a small group of Hebrew people in Britain around A.D. 100. However, the tradition states that they came to Glastonbury from the South after sailing down a river inlet. After about 400 years of the former Hebrews' influence on the Celtic culture, the Anglo-Saxons arrived, either absorbing many aspects of the cultures they found there, or replacing them with their own.

Consider the fact that the Anglo-Saxons came from lands to the North, much like the Tuatha de Danaan. These people brought with them, and impressed upon their new lands, their traditions and beliefs. To that end, imagine what they would have thought if they had arrived in Britain and discovered the community at Glastonbury claiming to be of Hebrew descent. To these invading northmen, this group must have confirmed their own legendary tales of Hebrew origin.

Likewise the question of the Tuatha coming to Britain from lands to the north is answered. They did indeed come to Britain from the north, but not in body. The Tuatha de Danaan of Celtic legend most likely arrived in the form of oral storytelling and foreign tradition brought by the invading Anglo-Saxons. These people who came from the region of Denmark, the "Land of the Tribe of Dan," had carried the legendary origins of their own people with them when they found those who followed the teaching of Joseph's church, or some form of it, and spoke of its origins in the distant land of Israel many years before.

The legend of the Hallows must also have tasted the salting the Anglo-Saxon influence gave to the Celtic culture. From it comes four of the Treasures of Britain—the spear, the sword, the cauldron, and the stone of Faill. All these magical items were said to have come from lands to the north with the Tuatha de Danaan. For this reason, one may surmise that if the tale of the Tuatha de Danaan came from the Anglo-Saxons encountering the descendants of the original Hebrew members of the church at Glastonbury, the legend of the "magical" relics held by the Tuatha may be the result of the same conquerors encountering real objects, either in the possession of the people at Glastonbury, or central to their traditions at the time. If these Nordic people, who imagined themselves to be descendants of a lost Hebrew tribe, thought the Glastonbury church members were those who would later be called the Tuatha de Danaan, it is likely that the "Treasures" ascribed to the Tuatha were the same Hallows associated with the Grail (which were at Joseph's church at Glastonbury. From this it follows that the Tuatha de Danaan are the mislabeled followers of the church at Glastonbury; and the treasures of Celtic mythology were real objects of veneration to those church members.

If these Norse invaders found a group of people living in the lands of Britain claiming to be descended from the Hebrew homeland, this would have undoubtedly reminded them of their own legends to the same effect. However, would this have been fuel enough to start the fire that became the Tuatha legend in Ireland? If Joseph and his party did burn the boats in which they arrived on the shores of Britain, knowing they couldn't return to Israel, would this have been enough to evolve over time into the misty origins of the Fairy Folk—or was there something else that aided this evolution?

Consider one important factor. The Tribe of Dan, traveling through ancient Europe, was called "Pelasgians" by some. With this in mind, an incredible coincidence links the Tribe of Dan to the small community of Hebrew descendants at Glastonbury. Those who claimed to be the true heirs to the legacy of Christ's church were those who followed the teachings of a man named Pelagius, and were thus to history labeled "Pelagians."

5

The Pelagian Heresy
and the British Church

The history of western culture is filled with confused, mixed traditions. It seems the world we live in was built upon the wreckage of past power struggles and conflicting ideals. Change was not usually implemented slowly in the ancient world. After every significant disturbance, whether it be war, a power vacuum, or an alteration in beliefs, came a period in which different factions jockeyed for the top position. So was the history of the political world, and so was the history of the Christian world as well.

After the death of Christ, His followers spread across Europe, endeavoring to take the new Christian teachings to different lands. During the early decades of the newborn Christian church came an unbelievable mingling of traditions where Christianity met these distant cultures. Christian holidays were made to fit into existing cultures' belief systems—days such as Valentine's Day, All Saint's Day, and Christmas. Nowhere was this mingling more colorfully demonstrated than in the joining of Christian philosophy and the pagan beliefs of the Celts. In the following poem, *The Dream of the Rood*, the nature-based traditions of the Celts and the reverence of Christianity meet in the wooden grain of the Cross.

> Behold, I will tell of a dream
> that came to me at midnight when
> those who talk are occupied with bed.
> I thought I saw a wondrous tree
> reaching high and circled
> with light of the brightest beams.
> That sign was covered in gold;

gems stood out where it met
the earth with five more higher up.
All the Lord's angels, fair for all time,
beheld it. This was no criminal's gallows;
these were holy angels watching,
and all men, and all creation.

Rare was that cross
I was outlawed by sin,
wounded with wrongdoing.
I saw that glorious tree
wrapped in a shining
garment, dressed in gold;
gems wrapped it well,
that tree of the Lord.

Through the gold, though, I saw
an old, wretched agony: it began
to bleed on the right side.
I was troubled by sorrow, afraid
of what I saw. I saw that sign
change clothes and color: sometimes
covered with moisture, drenched in
blood; sometimes arrayed in treasure
    [lines 1–23].

They pierced me with dark nails:
the wounds are plain to see,
horrible open wounds. I dared do
no harm to them. They mocked us
both. I was streaming with blood,
covered with blood from that man's side
after he sent forth his spirit.
I endured bitter things on that hill:
I saw the hosts of God tortured.
Darkness covered the Ruler's corpse,
that bright radiance; shadow went forth,
dark under the clouds. All creation wept,
wailed the King's death:
Christ was on the cross [lines 46–56].

The Dream of the Rood is rich with references likening the Tree (the Cross) with the body of Christ, as well as other pagan–Christian comparisons. To fully appreciate this blending of traditions, one must carefully read the work in its entirety.

Created by an anonymous writer, this poem can be found in the tenth century *Vercelli Book*, but the story itself is certainly older. A segment of the text can be seen in the 8th century Ruthwell Cross of Northumbria.

The Dream of the Rood was written in Old English, the Anglo-Saxon dialog of Dark-Age Britain. In it, one sees the Celtic characteristic of the old wood "tree" of the cross experiencing agony and talking to the dreamer, while Christian metaphors appear via the glory and resplendency of the gilded, jeweled cross.

The early church saw more than curious imagery and poetry as a result of these mixing cultures. There were also a number of sects, or "heretical groups," trying to gain support during this time, not the least of which were the sects cumulatively known as the "Gnostics." In an attempt to create some order in the Christian faith—and some would say to draw together what would become the Roman Catholic Church—the Council of Nicea met in A.D. 325 to define what it meant to be "Christian." Although many topics were discussed during these meetings, the desired end was met in the form of the following document, called the "Nicene Creed."

> We believe (I believe) in one God, the Father Almighty, maker of heaven and earth, and of all things visible and invisible. And in one Lord Jesus Christ, the only begotten Son of God, and born of the Father before all ages. (God of God) light of light, true God of true God. Begotten not made, consubstantial to the Father, by whom all things were made. Who for us men and for our salvation came down from heaven. And was incarnate of the Holy Ghost and of the Virgin Mary and was made man; was crucified also for us under Pontius Pilate, suffered and was buried; and the third day rose again according to the Scriptures. And ascended into heaven, sits at the right hand of the Father, and shall come again with glory to judge the living and the dead, of whose Kingdom there shall be no end. And (I believe) in the Holy Ghost, the Lord and Giver of life, who proceeds from the Father (and the Son), who together with the Father and the Son is to be adored and glorified, who spoke by the Prophets. And one holy, catholic, and apostolic Church. We confess (I confess) one baptism for the remission of sins. And we look for (I look for) the resurrection of the dead and the life of the world to come. Amen.

It was the hope of this council that their meeting, as well as this document, would create one unified Christian Church, making clear what was accepted as the true practice and beliefs of the church, and what was seen as heretical.

This union did not last, however. Due to a confrontation between King Philip IV of France and Pope Boniface VIII, an unprecedented period of division in the Catholic Church (known as "the Great Schism") occurred from 1305 to 1416 when the Papacy moved from Rome to Avignon in France. Although the official headquarters of the Roman Catholic Church moved back again to Rome, the effects of this division were felt long afterward, and are said to have played a role in the Reformation.

This was not the first instance of a rivalry between two separate churches, both claiming to be the "true" church of the Christian faith. In A.D. 380, a man by the name of Pelagius left his native Britain and journeyed to Rome to claim that the church at Glastonbury, founded by Joseph of Arimathea, was the first church built in the name of Christianity, and therefore deserved to be recognized as the more correct apostolic branch along which the church should follow. Not surprisingly, this claim was not well received by the Pope in Rome, leading to Palagius' eventual excommunication and labeling as a heretic.

> From Vatican records we know that during the early fifth century the Church in Britain was preaching an alternative apostolic succession. Known as Pelagianism (after one of its exponents, Pelagius), it dared to question the authority of the Roman popes. Although most records of their doctrine were destroyed, it is possible that the Pelagians believed that their succession descended from Joseph of Arimathea. Two fourth-century documents in the Vatican, the *Evangelium Nicodemi* and the *Vindicta Salvatoris*, demonstrate that early Christians in the pre–Catholic empire considered Joseph of Arimathea to be the first leader of Christ's Church. The *Vindicta Salvatoris* even suggests that Joseph was believed to have founded his Church in Britain [*The Search for the Grail*, Graham Phillips, p. 53].

Little else is known about this man Pelagius. Inasmuch as history can illuminate his life, Pelagius was born around 354 and died in 418, soon after the Synod of Jerusalem declared him a heretic in 415. The reasons for his conflict with the church and subsequent excommunication are understandable. His doctrine included ideas antithetical to Christian tradition, such as the thought that Adam did not pass on his "original sin," thus making all mankind who followed him free of any sin except that which he placed upon himself. Also, Pelagius suggested that Jesus did not die on the cross to rid all mankind of their sin, but rather that He died simply as a result of man's ignorance and turning away from the simple life of virtue that He followed. In other words, Pelagius and his followers, the heirs to the Joseph-of-Arimathea-tradition at Glastonbury, believed that Jesus was not the son of God, and was instead a perfect example of the sin-free life all people could achieve if only they tried. However, one of Pelagius' most interesting tenets was that the Mosaic Laws (or laws of the Old Testament) were as good a guide for living as the Gospels of the New Testament.

Described as a tall but portly man, Pelagius is said to have been well-educated, and able to speak and write fluently in Greek and Latin. After arriving in Rome, he spent many years there, according to St. Augustine, living in the city for "a very long time" [*Catholic Encyclopedia*, "Pelagius and Pelagianism"]. During that time he apparently befriended a man by the name of Caelestius, who found virtue and guidance in the monastic life as set forth by Pelagius.

Thanks in no small part to Caelestius' act of making his mentor's ideas for spiritual purity into a formal doctrine, their presence and unorthodox claims began to cause a stir in Rome. Although the Pelagian message was not well received, the two did not feel the weight of their views until they left Rome and journeyed to the shores of North Africa near Hippo. While Pelagius and Caelestius were not physically harmed for their doctrine, they continued to make enemies.

Finally, when Pelagius left Africa to travel to Palestine, his teachings were ruled a heresy, and he and Caelestius were excommunicated. Although this decision was overturned when Pelagius brought the case before Zosimus, the Council of Ephesus again ruled against him, once and for all separating this British lay-monk from the Roman Catholic Church, and branding Pelagianism a heresy.

One may wonder how the church founded by Joseph of Arimathea, the founder of the Grail legend in Britain, could become a church in which Jesus was seen simply as a model for a clean a virtuous life. It would seem that either Pelagius was not truly of this group of Christians at Glastonbury, or that this chapel founded on sanctity and the housing and protection of Christian relics fell from its previous holy state. To understand the role Pelagius played in the history of the Grail Hallows, it is necessary to explore the foundation of his unusual beliefs.

One must remember that when Joseph and his followers arrived at Glastonbury, they did so as a particular branch of the Jewish religion. There was no Christian church at this time. Christianity was seen as a "reformed" version of Judaism. Although the followers of Jesus had just witnessed something spectacular in His resurrection, they still held deep-seated Judaic beliefs. Therefore, it is understandable why Pelagius claimed that the Laws of Moses were as good a yardstick against which to measure one's worth as the teachings of Jesus. During His ministries, Jesus said, "Think not that I am come to destroy the law, or the prophets: I am not come to destroy, but to fulfill" [*The Holy Bible*, KJV, Matthew 5:17].

The Letters of Pelagius and His Followers reveals this specific side of the Pelagian way of thinking. In the first paragraph of his letter to Demetrias— a fourteen-year-old virgin who, upon being forced into marriage with an Italian refugee, professes a vow of chastity—the most important of the Pelagian views are expressed.

Even if I could claim to possess natural talent of a high quality and an equally high degree of artistic skill and believed myself for that reason to be capable of fulfilling with ease the obligation of writing, I would still not be able to enter upon this arduous task without considerable fear of the difficulties involved. It is to Demetrias that I have to write, that virgin of Christ who is both noble and rich and, which is more important, spurns both nobility and riches; assuredly it is as difficult for me to instruct her as it is easy for all to praise her out of admiration for her outstanding virtue. Who could possibly lack words to sing the praises of one who, though born in the highest station, brought up in the height of wealth and luxury, held fast by the strength and variety of this life's delights as if in the grip of the most tenacious of fetters, suddenly broke free and exchanged all her bodily goods simultaneously for goodness of the soul? Of one who cut off with the sword of faith, that is, her own free will, the very flower of a life still only just beginning and, by crucifying her flesh with Christ, dedicated it as a living and holy sacrifice to God and for love of virginity renounced the prospect of providing posterity for a very noble stock? An easy, simple way to make a speech is to let the very richness of the subject-matter speed it along its course; but we have to proceed along a very different road, since our purpose is to write a manual of instruction for the virgin, not an encomium, to portray not so much the virtues which she has already acquired as those which she has still to acquire, and to order the remainder of her life rather than to honour that part of it which is now in the past [*The Letters of Pelagius and his Followers*, B. R. Rees, pp. 35–36].

In the opening of his letter to the "virgin of Christ," Pelagius states quite clearly what is important to him in a devotee: simplicity, humility, poverty, and virginity (or at least abstinence).

Later in his treatise to Demetrias, he quotes Second Peter from the New Testament in the same paragraph as Hebrews and Psalms. Again, in another paragraph, he pairs the book of Romans with the book of Leviticus. Throughout the letters of not only Pelagius but also those who would call themselves Pelagians, this type of mating of Old and New Testaments proliferates. From these passages one can see that Pelagius had not so deeply ingrained a Christian philosophym so much as a Hebrew outlook with a Christian flavoring.

The previous passage contains one possible bit of foreshadowing. Pelagius speaks of his desire to "write a manual of instruction." Here lies the connection between Pelagius and research into the history of the Grail Hallows. It may be that the later followers of Pelagius did in fact write a book outlining not only his teachings, but also certain historical markers having to do with the Hallows. This book, created in an unusual form, has been passed down through history, through the hands of this early heretical sect in Britain, through the hands of the Albegensian Cathars, to us today, not as a book, but as an early version of common gaming cards—the deck of cards known as the Tarot.

6

Merlin and Blaise

When one begins a historical study of the Grail legend and the Hallows, the ever-present specter of mysticism looms over any attempt to find fact in myth. One need only mention "King Arthur" or "Grail" in the company of historians to discover that these topics are not seen as valid investigations of history. For this reason, there can be no more uncertain ground on which to tread than to look at the Arthurian character of Merlin from a historical standpoint. "Merlin the Magician" is known the world over— seen as an old man in a conical hat, wearing a long, purple robe covered in stars and crescent moons, wielding magic with a glowing wand gripped firmly in his ancient hands.

This image of Merlin lends itself to the notion that the stories of Arthur, the Grail, and the Hallows are nothing but fanciful tales created by the minds of medieval writers. Popular culture has not aided in the dissolution of this image, given its creation of electronic games named after the mythical character, or a television series about a modern-day Merlin who, owning a garage and service station, finds the reincarnated King Arthur in the form of a boy who pulls an enchanted crowbar out of a cement-filled bucket. Society clings to its imagery so dearly that it is not expected, and even unwelcome, for one to look for reality in such characters.

As unlikely as it may seem, Merlin the magician, boon to Arthur and knower of the ancient ways, appears to be based on a true historical character. However, to understand this man, one must first forget the robes, the hat, and the magic wand, and rediscover him as a man, or possibly two men, who were simply people of their time who served, believed, and acted as many others did in that period. The image of Merlin as we know him seems to have come from the combining of two different historical figures—

one named Merlinus, and another named Myrddin Wilt, or Merlin the Wild.

To understand who Merlin really was, one must first consider the time period involved. If Merlin was contemporary with King Arthur, that would place him in the fifth to sixth century A.D. It is thought that the Battle of Camlaan, at which Arthur dies, was fought in A.D. 552; and if Merlin was an old man at the time, he was probably born in the latter half of the fifth century. One may then wonder if any such man named Merlin was mentioned at about that time period, which would place him alongside the renowned King Arthur.

The first mention of Merlin as being Arthur's advisor came from Geoffrey of Monmouth's twelfth-century work, *History of the Kings of Britain*. Monmouth is noted as being one of the first historians to detail the events and battles of King Arthur's life. It has been thought that Geoffrey simply took the tradition of the Welsh prophet named Myrddin and changed his name from its normal Latinized form, "Merdinus," to "Merlinus," since the first form sounded much like the Anglo-Saxon word "merde," which meant "excrement." However, many historians now believe Geoffrey's Merlinus was a Christianized Briton who lived from A.D. 450 to 536.

The first historical Merlin, Merlinus, appears to have been born in the Welsh area known as Caermarthen to the Royal Princess of Dyfed. Although something is known of Merlin's mother, apparently the identity of Merlin's father was not only a mystery, but a curse, for many thought his father to be the devil himself. Norma Lorre Goodrich said the following about Merlin's name and heritage in her book *Merlin*.

> Another version is that Merlin's name was rooted in the Latin comparative *Melius* or *Melior* (better) because he declared himself the son of the world's best mother, *Optima*. No other name in Latin has been as widely recorded for Merlin's mother, and mother and son had in French no husband/father, but only a father confessor named Blaise [p. 29].

Although it is important to know the name of Merlin's mother, *Optima* (whether it be her proper name or a descriptive name), it will become more important in later chapters to remember the name of his mother's priest and confessor, Blaise.

Because Merlin's mother could not name his father, the court accused her of fornication. However, the young Merlin stepped forward and clearly stated the identity of his father, and how he came to be as he was. He claimed that his father was none other than the Devil by way of an incubus that seduced his mother while she slept. According to Merlin, the

Devil's plan was to use Merlin as an evil version of Christ on earth. Luck-ily this plan was thwarted, Merlin said, when his mother's confessor swept him up and baptized him, cleansing Merlin of his evil, but leaving him invested with powers of second sight as a by-product of his supernatural creation.

Legend states that just such a boy, who was the son of no man, was needed to help build a strong foundation for a castle stronghold being con-structed for the Saxon warlord Vortigern. However, the assistance needed was not Merlin's second sight or insights into the failures they had previ-ously encountered. What Vortigern's soothsayers needed from Merlin was his own sacrificial blood. Calling the warlord's wizards fools, Merlin showed the mighty warlord the source of his fortress' problems. Merlin lead them all down to an underground pool beneath the mountain on which the fortress was being constructed, and stated that the reason the walls kept falling in was due to a great battle taking place beneath the water between a red and a white dragon.

Merlin said he saw a vision of the red dragon driving the white dragon back across the sea. In retrospect, it seems clear that Merlin meant the red dragon to represent the Britons, and the white dragon to represent the Sax-ons. Staying true to his prophet legacy, this vision would indeed come true. Vortigern would fall to the sword of Ambrosius Aurelianus, who later passed the British throne to Uther Pendragon, father of King Arthur, who was finally successful in repelling the Saxons.

This was not the end of Merlin's story, however. According to the twelfth century *Vita Merlini*, Merlin went north after the death of King Arthur, where he fell into the service of King Gwendoleu and took the name Llallogan. After some time, Gwendoleu went to war with King Rid-erch Hael of Strathclyde, and Kings Peredyr and Gwrgi, both of York. Dur-ing the battle, King Gwedoleu was killed. As a result of his lord's death, Merlin is thought to have gone insane and retreated into the forests nearby.

Although Geoffrey of Monmouth claimed the Merlin he called Mer-linus was the same Merlin who later was called Myrddin Wilt after becom-ing a madman of the forest, Arthurian historian and writer Norma Lorre Goodrich states that Myrddin was a different man altogether. Since the bat-tle of Ardderyd between Gwedoleu and his enemies occurred in 573, Mer-lin would have to have died at the ripe old age of 123 if Merlinus and Myrddin Wilt were the same man. While the Merlin of lore could have conjured a potion to prolong his life, a historical personage would have died at a much younger age indeed.

The historical Merlin fell victim to the same type of forced association and erroneous claims of relation as did Arthur after his death. According to Goodrich, to simply encounter the name "Merlinus" or "Myrddin" in history doesn't mean one has found a reference to the great man himself.

> But Merlin seems to have belonged to all Wales and all Scotland rather than to one kingdom alone. He has strong ties to Carmarthen (Caerfyrddin) in Dyfed, where he was perhaps born, as well as to Powys and the Brecon (Brycheiniog) area, which was settled by his ancestral tribe, that of Brychan. On the other hand, the "Myrddin" to whom Taliesin is said to have referred was one of Merlin's self-styled heirs. Such a famous man has followers, especially among the mad [Goodrich, p. 179].

It would appear that, mad or sane, the Merlin of history had his "continuators," as did Chretien de Troyes. In this manner, the story of Merlin was changed by those who came after him—continued by people who knew his story, but played it out in their own way.

> Other men soon would be so affected by his legend that they roamed the forests of Scotland, King Arthur's same "Caledonian Forest," calling themselves "Myrddin," Merlin's name in British, as in modern Welsh [Goodrich, p. 265].

It is for this reason that Goodrich posits that Merlin of history is Merlinus of Arthur's time, and the "imposter" or madman was another individual named Myrddin Wilt. This very splitting of the Merlin tradition may explain the Celtic nature of the Grail Hallows story, which has lead to the assumption that the legend is entirely a Christianized Celtic myth. If this second Merlin, roaming mad through the Welsh and Scottish countryside, imagined himself to be the Merlin that aided Arthur, he would have surely passed on the Grail story as he knew it, likely with a Celtic flavor.

If this Merlin passed on the Grail legend through Celtic tradition, one must wonder what he knew of the relics in his time. Also, if he were not truly the Merlin of Arthurian legend, how would he have known the story at all? The answer is from a recent book allegedly written about it. It is here that one must remember the all-important reference to his mother's priest, Blaise, also called Blois or Blayse. According to the *Prose Merlin*, it is Blois who first writes the story of the Grail and, one must assume, the Hallows, as it was dictated to him by the young Merlin.

If Merlin can be considered the first Grail historian, and Blaise the first Grail romance writer, it is intriguing to think of what that first Grail text contained. If one believes the accounts given by Robert de Boron, who wrote about both the Grail and Merlin, Blaise would surely have written about the Grail's arrival with Joseph of Arimathea—only Joseph's Grail was said to have been two vials, not one cup. But was that the whole story as Blaise and Merlin knew it, or was there more to tell in this historical text? Since, according to Goodrich, Merlinus lived between 450 and 536, one may assume that he and Blaise also knew of the arrival of the Marian Chalice, the cup found by Helena in Christ's tomb, when it arrived in Britain from Rome in 410 AD. Therefore, it must be assumed that Blaise also wrote of this second vessel's coming to Britain, most likely to the ancient church of Joseph at Glastonbury. This event must have been seen as a great honor bestowed upon Glastonbury, having been picked by the church in Rome to house this relic for safe keeping. For this reason, one may expect to read in history books of the Roman church's fondness of its "sister church" in Britain. However, history records anything but this.

In researching the church in Britain in the fifth and sixth centuries, it becomes clear that the church in Rome considered itself to be the one and only church of Christ, while the church in Britain housed a heretical sect known as the Pelagians. As previously mentioned, Pelagius of Britain went to Rome preaching a doctrine that seemed to fly in the face of what the Roman Church had been saying for centuries.

Although the rift between the Roman Church and the Pelagian church in Britain is only one of several that would occur throughout history, it is important to remember that Pelagius based his claims of rightful succession to the Christian church on the British branch's founding by Joseph, and on the possession of the Grail. In fact, their history of Joseph and the Grail was of paramount importance to them, and served as a basis for their doctrine. They believed in Jesus as much as in the prophets of the Old Testament (as Joseph would have), and they remained aloof from doctrine originated by the Roman Catholic Church, such as the concept of original sin.

Since Merlin, as a Romanized Briton, gave credit for his prophetic powers to Christ and chose to tell the story of the Grail Hallows to the priest Blaise, it is reasonable to think that Merlin was familiar with, if not a member of, the Pelagian church in Britain. Since Pelagius had left for Rome nearly a hundred years before Merlin's birth, and the Marian Chalice had arrived in Britain a mere forty years prior to his birth, Merlin may have chosen this opportunity to honor the British legacy of Joseph and the Grail, along with the story of Pelagius, as part of this early "Grail history book" in defiance of the Roman excommunication of Pelagius and his followers in 416.

The British church's history is actually quite full of important events in the years between 380 and the end of the sixth century. Besides Pelagius' eventful encounter with the Roman Church and the birth of Merlinus, another figure of historical significance makes an appearance at Glastonbury during this time. Tradition states that the renowned St. Patrick visited the church at Glastonbury in the middle of the fifth century A.D., after his ministry in Ireland around 433. It is said that he came to the small community at Glastonbury, and found a tiny settlement of lay-monks living around what they claimed to be the original church founded by Joseph of Arimathea. However, by this time the ancient wattle church was in poor condition.

> There he found the twelve successors of Joseph at their post, but the "Old Chirche" required rebuilding; the wattles were worn out, but the sanctuary had become exceedingly sacred [*Central Somerset Gazette Official Guide to Glastonbury*, p. 8].

Glastonbury history states that the wattle church, or "Old Chirche," did at some time fall into disrepair, and that it was later covered by a protective shell of boards and tin. Since St. Patrick reportedly arrived to see the wattle church in this state, it is most likely that the wattle church by then was covered with its shell of boards and tin. In fact, this tin-covered version of the wattle church would later be protected by a stone church erected around and over it.

Unfortunately, all remains of the Old Chirche built by Joseph in the first century were destroyed when a catastrophic fire swept through Glastonbury Abbey in 1184. However, the current site of the Lady Chapel and St. Joseph's Crypt now rests on the site where the wattle church once stood.

This time period also yields the name of another "prophet" of some acclaim in Britain. Maelgwn, or Melkin, described as being one "who was before Merlin," was allegedly King of Gwynedd and Guinevere's cousin. He is important to the study of both Merlin and the Grail Hallows because he purportedly discovered the location of both the Hallows and the burial place of Joseph of Arimathea. In his introduction to *Perlesvaus: or the High History of the Holy Grail*, translator Sebastian Evans makes mention not only of a man who sounds quite like Melkin, but also a passage from *Fulke le Fitz-Warine* that speaks of "the book of the holy vessel."

Evans points out that in the "Chronicle of Helinand," one passage, dating from A.D. 720, speaks of a marvelous vision, revealed by an angel, to "... a certain hermit in Britain concerning S. Joseph, the decurion who deposed from the cross the Body of Our Lord, as well as concerning the paten or dish in the which Our Lord supped with His disciples, whereof the history was written out by the said hermit and is called 'Of the Graal' (de Gradali)."

Another citation in a medieval history emphasizes the importance of this passage. Although the "Chronicle of Helinand" apparently places this occurrence in the year 720, the events it describes sounds exactly like the account of Melkin finding the Hallows and Joseph's tomb, as well as mentioning the book he wrote about their discovery—a book John Leland dated to 450 and records seeing in the library at Glastonbury in 1534 in his *De Rebus Britannicis Collectanea*.

The Melkin manuscript includes a cryptic description of the whereabouts of Joseph's tomb.

> Joseph of Arimathea, the noble decurion, received his everlasting rest with his eleven associates in the Isle of Avalon. He lies in the Southern angle of the bifurcated line of the Oratorium of the Adorable Virgin. He has with him the two white vessels of silver which were filled with the blood and the sweat of the great Prophet Jesus.

From this description, it would seem that Melkin does the same thing as the "certain hermit in Britain" described in the "Chronicle of Helinand." He describes the location of at least some of the relics, and the location of Joseph's tomb. It is therefore almost certain that the entry dated 720 in the "Chronicle of Helinand" actually refers to the man Melkin, "who was before Merlin," and his book (which John Leland dated from A.D. 450).

The description given by Melkin sounds peculiar, but a little investigation uncovers the fact that the "Southern angle of the bifurcated line of the Oratorium of the Adorable Virgin" simply refers to the south corner of the Lady Chapel at Glastonbury. It is here where the crypt of St. Joseph can be found in the lower level of the Lady Chapel. In fact, the altar in the crypt rests right under the side of the Lady Chapel where tradition states the original altar of the wattle church once stood. Therefore, Joseph's crypt and tomb would have been buried outside the eastern wall of the small wattle building that served as the Old Chirche, very near the well that once stood some feet in front of the wattle church, and now is part of the Lady Chapel's southern wall.

The references made by the "Chronicle of Helinand" do not stop there, however. In fact, Sebastian Evans goes even further to outline the relevance between the "Chronicle" and the "Book of the Graal," which he perceives to be a type of sourcebook with which the author of the "Chronicle" must be familiar.

> On the first page of the Romance, Helinand read that an Angel had appeared to a certain hermit in Britain and revealed to him the history of the Holy Graal. In transferring the record of this event to his "Chronicle," he was compelled by the exigencies of his system, which required the insertion of every event recorded under some particular

year, to assign a date to the occurrence. A vague "five hundred years ago" would be likely to suggest itself as an appropriate time at which the occurrence might be supposed to have taken place; and if he were writing in 1220, the revelation to the hermit would thus naturally be relegated to the year 720, the year under which the entry actually appears. This, of course, is pure guesswork, but the fact remains that the "Chronicle" was written in or about 1220, and the "Book of the Graal" not long before it.

Evans asserts that the "Book of the Graal" must have been written not long before the "Chronicle" because Helinand had difficulty obtaining a copy of the "Book of the Graal" for his review. Evans states that the book must have been recently written, or else copies of the "Book of the Graal" would have been plentiful.

However, this assumption is only one possible reason of many why Helinand could not obtain a copy of this manuscript. It is not necessarily true that a medieval text's scarcity indicates that it had yet to be copied. Further, Evans mentions an intriguing clue about the manuscript's author that points again to a much earlier date.

> The name of the author is nowhere recorded. He may possibly be referred to in the "Elucidation" prefixed to the rhymed version of "Percival le Gallois" under the name of "Master Blihis," but this vague and tantalizing pseudonym affords no hint of his real identity.

One cannot hear a name like "Master Blihis" in relation to the author of a mysterious "Book of the Graal" without thinking of Blaise and the history of the Grail he wrote at the behest of Merlinus in the fifth century.

It seems likely that the mysterious character of Merlin played a vital role in the development of the Hallows legend. Not only does it seem that Merlin was a historical figure, it appears he was the first Grail Romancer, if not the first Grail text author. Through his knowledge of the Grail Hallows, one can surmise that he was familiar with the history of Joseph of Arimathea and his relics, as well as the tradition of Pelagius and the arrival of the Marian Chalice at the church of Britain at Glastonbury. Further, the tradition of Merlin dictating the history of the Hallows to Blaise seems supported by the "Chronicles of Helinand" and the mysterious "Book of the Graal" mentioned therein. It also seems most likely that its author, "Master Blihis," and Merlin's transcriber, Blaise, are one in the same.

This offers an image of Merlin far different from the popular character of fantasy. One can envision Merlin, with the help of Blaise, standing over a scriptorium bench, dutifully penning a manuscript that would in some form become the sourcebook used by later medieval authors to create the now famous legend of the Grail and the Hallows. However, one may question how this original sourcebook evolved and traveled through history to become the legend with which most are now familiar. Thanks to medieval monks, endlessly toiling in the transcription and copying of such old texts, the world has many examples of these ancient stories to read to this day.

7

The Book

Life today is easy, at least more so than it was a thousand years ago. Today we have the Internet linking the world together, sharing media and knowledge freely and easily. Without leaving one's desk, it is possible to read the latest work being done in the field of nuclear medicine, or a translation of an ancient manuscript. Unfortunately, this also means that one can read about how to make a bomb from fertilizer, or maintain ties to terrorists, or connect with other hate groups. Fundamentally, information has always been of great worth. Paradoxically, it has also always been cause for great fear.

It goes without saying that the oldest format offering recorded information is the book. A book, whether bound pages, scrolls, or a carved wall, can be described, even by the most cynical, as something magical. Books hold the words and thoughts and emotions of someone who is not there to speak them personally. That means that one may be, in a sense, hearing the voice of someone who has long since perished. It has been said that words are cheap, but consider the fact that some words have changed worlds, built dynasties, and torn them down. Words have created gods, not to mention enraged those who would speak for their god.

Books have been burned—supposedly in the name of righteousness, as they have been for the sake of evil. Books, throughout history, have been the most venomous of pets, inspiring both love and dreadful fear in the hearts and minds of those who keep them. It is this paradox that plays a key role in a book written by Umberto Eco called *The Name of the Rose*. In this book, murders plague a remote monastery, prompting the visitation of a Franciscan monk and investigator, William of Baskerville, and his somewhat less well-read protégé, Adso. Being described as one who is,

"...familiar with the ways of the evil one [the devil]," William is expected to discover what is causing the mysterious deaths in their holy order. However, being somewhat more pragmatic, William sees nothing more than a crime scene, one posing more questions than answers.

As the story plays out, the murders come not at the hands of the devil, but at the hands of the victims themselves. Certain tell-tell characteristics appear on the bodies of the murdered monks—their fingers and tongues are found to be blackened. Their deaths were dealt by their own hand when they licked their fingers to turn the next poisoned page in a book forbidden by their order. This Greek book spoke of humor and laughing—something heavily frowned upon by the monastery's eldest member, the venerable Jorge.

Jorge keeps the forbidden book in a vast labyrinthine library, which, when secretly entered by William of Baskerville, causes William's heart to leap with joy. His eyes had never beheld such wondrous books held therein. When William finally finds the poisoned tome, with the blind Jorge hovering over it like a dark vulture, he sees the "profane" book for the beautiful work it is. However, his encounter with the book is brief. Jorge, realizing this is a man he could not so easily silence, flees with the book, causing a disastrous fire in the process. The climax of *The Name of the Rose* comes when William emerges from the smoke and flames clutching the few treasured works that he could save from the burning tower.

Although this sequence demonstrates the worst side of man's relationship with books, one quote from the subsequent film based on the book concisely describes the role of the medieval book copier. In a speech given by the venerable Jorge the night before William finds the forbidden tome, Jorge states his view of the monk-transcribers' duty.

> Let us return to what was, and ever should be, the office of this abbey—the preservation of knowledge. "Preservation" I say, not "search for." Because there is no progress in the history of knowledge, merely continuous and sublime recapitulation [*The Name of the Rose*, 20th Century–Fox, 1986].

To fully appreciate the value of an ancient manuscript, such as that of Blaise's history of the Grail Hallows, one must first understand how such manuscripts survived the ordeal of time and changing social values to the modern day. To do so, one must not only understand the role of the medieval scribe, sitting in his cold scriptorium, but also in what manner such a text would have been written.

Books were not always items one could find at every turn. It has only been since the invention of the printing press that the written word has become so readily available. Anything put into writing that was not an inventory, a military enrollment list, or some other mundane document of civilization was done either as an act of great scholarship, or at the behest of a patron who paid for its creation. Therefore, the modern reader must realize that most of the great works of antiquity were true labors of love— not just love of the subject matter, but love of the book itself.

Keeping this in mind will serve to counteract the common tendency to trivialize histories written before what is considered the "modern age." What appears to the twenty-first-century eye to be colorful elaboration and mystical decoration when reading an early text is simply a look into the perception of the mind that created it. One must remember that the process of writing was not one entered into lightly in ancient times. One had to be cautious at best, and secretive at worst. After all, what is now known as basic physics was considered a heresy, and earned a death sentence for the man who first deciphered and wrote down its laws.

Besides the political and philosophical dangers a writer faced when creating a text in ancient times, writing anything of any great length was very labor intensive. The earliest writings are found in the form of carvings, whether they be on a clay tablet or a stone monument. To write by creating an indentation in a medium physically strong enough to last was a very difficult task. Imagine having to sit down to write a relative or create a budgetary report for your supervisor if you had to write it entirely with a stick and a box of semi-dried mud. Or imagine having to write your feelings about a departed loved one using a wooden mallet and a chisel.

However, if one limits such consideration about writing to the time period in question, that being the time from the late Roman era to the Middle Ages, the task of writing becomes somewhat easier. The concept of a *book* arose when man started creating his written works with pigment on a moveable medium. Scrolls made of animal skin, papyrus, or other materials were carried and passed around for many to read, allowing information to be more easily spread.

Archeologists have learned a great deal about ancient civilizations by the writings they left behind. A great many Greek and Roman texts have been found speaking about various aspects of their everyday life, allowing not only an invaluable insight into the minutest facet of their cultures, but a detailed outline of their histories. Similar records exist on the life and culture of their Hebrew counterparts. Recent history is full of discoveries of ancient texts dealing with this difficult intermingling of cultures and transitions of faith. Texts such as the Dead Sea Scrolls and the Nag Hammadi codices have shone a whole new light on a time period previously chronicled largely by the Bible alone.

While such newsworthy discoveries capture the minds and imaginations of thousands, the truth is that most of our view of the ancient world comes to us not from archeological discoveries, but from the dutiful hands of medieval monks whose job it was to ensure the continuation and preservation of original texts in their possession. In fact, it has been said that had it not been for these holy men, the western past would have been largely forgotten and lost to time.

Common perception of a medieval monastery envisions men in long brown robes slowly walking around all day muttering Gregorian Chants, pouring over their copies of the Bible, saying prayers, and leading a simple life. While this is true to an extent, the picture remains incomplete without the inclusion of a knife and quill. Many of these men who lived their life in dedication to God also recognized the importance of man's legacy to its own future. Although they would not be considered as such in the strictest sense today, these men of the church were writers, artists, and craftsmen of the highest caliber.

Called *antiquarii* (or antiquarians), these monk-transcribers created manuscripts that were retellings of ancient oral traditions, recreations of classical comedies and dramas, and reproductions of writings of such antiquity that they would surely have been lost had it not been for the scribes' efforts. In that regard, they were the first archeologists. Further, the books for which they are responsible were not simple reproductions. They were augmented by elaborate decorations called "illuminations," which ranged from ornate lettering to fanciful scenes—either of the text's subject matter or of the scribe's own creation.

When someone today sees these works of art, it is difficult to think of them as books—simple conglomerations of page and ink. It is often easy to overlook these books as sources of information, and become overwhelmed by the incredible beauty and workmanship involved. For the monks, however, this artwork was simple adornment for the real "meat and potatoes" of their work, a kind of diversion from the difficult task that faced them.

During the Middle Ages, monasteries possessed several very distinct features, both in their construction and in their function. Most monasteries were self-sufficient, enclosed institutions, much like a small city, with its members serving key offices. In that regard, the scriptorium could be considered the city's newspaper office or television news station. They were there to pass on information in the form of the day.

The process of making books was not easy by any means. It was not simply a matter of getting some paper, some pens, and setting to work. The paper had to be made, the ingredients to make the ink had to be grown and then mixed, and the feathers that made the pens had to be plucked from fowl raised on the premises. Likewise, the animals that provided the leather book-covers had to be raised, the pen-knives made, and so forth. With all this to do, book-making called on the skills and resources of the whole monastery's infrastructure. The Philadelphia Museum of Art and the Philadelphia Area Consortium of Special Collections Libraries are conducting a project entitled "Leaves of Gold: Treasures of Manuscript Illumination from Philadelphia Collections" that both beautifully details the process of medieval manuscript creation and exhibits some of the finest examples of Medieval illuminations. The following description of the manuscript creation process is based on resources pertaining to the "Leaves of Gold" project.

The whole process began with the paper on which to write. The "paper" wasn't paper at all, but animal skin called "parchment" or "vellum." The skins had to be soaked and scrubbed to clean off the animal's hair and then stretched out on a wooden frame, where it was scraped smooth. The skin would then be dusted with plaster to absorb any remaining residue and rubbed with a pumice stone to create a surface that would accept the ink. The skins were then dried to become the finished parchment. Anyone looking at a manuscript page made of parchment may actually see small holes in the page caused by the treatment process. Sometimes these flaws were used to the scribe's advantage, as they created decorative illustrations around the holes (such as peacock feathers, peering eyes, or the gaping mouths of fearful beasts meant to represent the open passage to Hell).

The next item to be made was the ink. Although monks employed many different colors of ink in the illuminations, the black ink used for the text itself was concocted either from crushed gallnuts, or lamp soot mixed with egg white. The other types of ink were made from any number of things (such as plants, minerals, and insects), ground to a powder form and mixed with egg white, or *egg glair*, to make the liquid ink.

When the page and ink were both ready to use, the process of copying the text in question began in earnest. First the scribe took the existing manuscript, or exemplar, and set it on a stand above his workspace. Next, he used a stylus to create rule lines on the vellum to keep the text straight on the page, allowing space for any illuminations or illustrations he wished to put on the page. The instrument he used for the actual writing was called a quill, made from a feather that had been sharpened down to a point (much like the nib on a modern fountain pen).

One of the last things put on a medieval manuscript page was the illuminations or any other type of artwork that was to accompany the text.

While most often this job was left to someone who specialized in illumination, it was sometimes done in conjunction with the writing of the text. One other form of adornment for these manuscripts was the use of thin gold leaf applied to the pages, either as part of the illumination, inside the text, or as a border surrounding the entire page. Books that included such gold leaf were considered to be of the highest quality.

The book's final stage of creation was the binding process, in which the loose pages were collected and sewn together at the spine. The spine was then attached to wooden boards covered in leather to form the front and back covers. It was at this stage that some books would be further augmented by shaped wooden blocks that formed raised panels and decorative features beneath the leather covering. Finally, clasps were attached to both covers so that the book could be held closed.

Obviously, the process of making a book required a great deal of dedication, not to mention a degree of artistry. The monks at these monasteries would spend each day at their scriptorium desks or in their rooms, or cells, copying hundreds of books in their lifetimes. If an individual showed a talent for the work, it would become their sole responsibility. To obtain some idea of the life the medieval transcriber led, the reader is invited to get a bottle of ink, sharpen a long feather into a point, and attempt to write by hand the words contained on this page. Now imagine having to copy the entirety of this book, and having to perform such an exercise for the rest of your life, and you'll understand how important books were to those who dedicated themselves to painstakingly copying the ancient texts that are readily available today at the local book store.

One group in particular did an especially good job at preserving western civilization through its ancient manuscripts. In his book *How the Irish Saved Civilization: The Untold Story of Ireland's Heroic Role from the Fall of Rome to the Rise of Medieval Europe*, Thomas Cahill asserts that Ireland's monasteries saved more important works of literature and other texts that defined western civilization than did any other group throughout history. It is important to realize that this is not a statement made by one man alone. Many historians agree that the survival of a great many of the important writings of man can be attributed to the work of the Irish monks during the Middle Ages.

When historians speak of the "Dark Ages" this is not necessarily the same as when they talk of the Middle Ages, although the former is contained within the latter. The Dark Ages refers to a time just after the fall of Rome. History often uses the civilizations of Greece and Rome to describe "golden ages" of western civilization. These were times in which important strides were made that are reflected in our way of life today, or that otherwise outline a way of life that could, for the time, be considered "as good as it gets." One term epitomizing this sentiment is the *Pax Romana*—the Roman "Age of Peace."

To the same degree that the *Pax Romana* embodied a golden age, the time just after the fall of Rome became the Dark Ages. One can liken this period to conditions portrayed in modern post-apocalyptic films such as *The Road Warrior*, in which roaming tribes of barbarians used fear and strength to legitimize their power. It was a time dedicated to basic survival itself, rather than the survival of ancient texts and wisdom. Of this time, and the threat to history itself, Cahill writes:

> Had the destruction been complete—had every library been disassembled and every book burned—we might have lost Homer and Virgil and all of classical poetry, Herodotus and Tacitus and all of classical history, Demosthenes and Cicero and all of classical oratory, Plato and Aristotle and all of Greek philosophy, and Plotinus and Porphyry and all the subsequent commentary. We would have lost the taste and smell of a whole civilization. Twelve centuries of lyric beauty, aching tragedy, intellectual inquiry, scholarship, sophistry, and love of Wisdom—the acme of ancient civilized discourse—would all have gone down the drain of history [*How the Irish Saved Civilization*, Cahill, p. 58].

To illustrate how the Irish were instrumental in preserving all that which might have been lost, Cahill demonstrates the great chasm that separated the Roman west and Ireland.

> By the end of the fourth century, if we are to believe one writer, Ammianus Marcellinus, who may be indulging in hyperbole, *"Bibliotecis sepulcrorum ritu in perpetuum clausis"* ("The libraries, like tombs, were closed forever") [Cahill, p. 182].

> Ireland, at peace and furiously copying, thus stood in the position of becoming Europe's publisher. But the pagan Saxon settlements of southern England had cut Ireland off from easy commerce with the continent. While Rome and its ancient empire faded from memory and a new, illiterate Europe rose on its ruins, a vibrant, literary culture was blooming in secret along its Celtic fringe [Cahill, p. 183].

Like green grass growing alongside a fence, fed by neglect and ignored until it took on a life of its own, the transcription tradition of Irish monasteries is responsible for the preservation of countless works of ancient thought and wisdom. The Celtic musical artist Loreena McKennitt has written a moving song entitled *Skellig* about the monks at the monastery that once sat atop the seven-hundred-foot peak on the isle of Skellig Michael, eighteen miles off the Irish coast. It was places such as this, Cahill

The Skellig Michael monastery is an austere spike of cold rock jutting out of the North Atlantic about 18 miles off the southern coast of Ireland. Here many great works of classical literature were copied and translated during the Middle Ages. It is thanks to the monks who dwelt in monasteries such as Skellig Michael that we have classics of ancient literature to read and ponder today. (Photograph courtesy of Des Lavelle Valentia, County Kerry, Ireland.)

says in the introduction to his book, to which western civilization clung in those dark times.

The reason medieval transcription is important to the history of the Grail Hallows is simple. It has been suggested that Merlin relayed the saga of the Grail Hallows to Blaise, who then wrote it down for the first time. If one is to believe that the modern legend of the Grail originated in Britain at Glastonbury with this early manuscript, it is important to see how such a manuscript could be preserved over the centuries so that a twelfth-century French writer could read this same manuscript, in some form, and transform it into the Grail legend as it exists today.

In the fourth and fifth centuries A.D., at the height of the Dark Ages, the legend of the Grail Hallows was born into the world of the written word. Along Europe's "Celtic fringe," the greatest story to come out of the Dark Ages was being kept under the watchful eyes of those who valued it the most. However, one may wonder how it came to be in the hands of Chretien de Troyes in the twelfth century, and why it had changed so much.

In the early Glastonbury community, during and just after the time of Joseph of Arimathea, the stories of the Grail and the other Hallows surely were passed on primarily through oral tradition. Life surrounding the Wattle church may have been monastic and reverent, but food still needed to be grown and animals raised for survival. The swell of thought surrounding the relics of Christ's Passion probably did not begin until after Joseph's death. In fact, it would appear that the community at Glastonbury fell into decline until Patrick's arrival around the middle of the fifth century having reached its peak before Pelagius left for Rome in A.D. 380.

Perhaps in honor of Pelagius' less-than-triumphant return to the British Isles, or perhaps due to Patrick's infusion of vigor into the Glastonbury community, or perhaps even for reasons simply lost to time, the legacy of Joseph and the Grail Hallows at Glastonbury did not go down the historical drain—thanks to Blaise, the first Grail writer. The text written about these relics developed into a mystery almost as deep as that of the Grail Hallows themselves. Statements made by the early medieval Grail romancers, such as Chretien de Troyes and Robert de Boron, indicate that they gleaned their knowledge about the Grail from a particular sourcebook. In some texts, the Grail is actually said to be, among other things, a book.

It is clear that the Grail called many things by many people, it is more than one simple relic, but how could it be a book? Possibly the very name for the relic lay at the root of the mystery. The Holy Grail was called the *Sangraal*, without any further explanation, until Robert de Boron elaborated on Chretien's story shortly after Chretien's death. The term "Sangraal" comes from the French *San Graal* (Holy Grail). One word that might have been used to describe the book of the Grail (if not by Blaise, then by someone who later read or elaborated on his manuscript) is "gradual," which means "prayer book." Therefore, if the book written by Blaise or a manuscript written by someone continuing Blaise's work, was called a prayer book, or gradual, it is possible that this book may have been entitled the "Holy Prayer Book" or, in French, "*San Gradual*."

But how could the term *San Gradual* be transformed into *Sangraal* (basically turning the story in a book into a story about a cup, the Holy Grail) in such a short period of time by a group of people who based their claim of being the true church of Christ on the history of their relics? Such a blurring of tradition, as well as several other confusions of historical events, leads one to believe that such changes to the original story of the Grail Hallows as written in the Blaise text must have been made by a group who came some time afterward (possibly hundreds of years afterward), and who simply "picked up" the writings and traditions of Pelagius and his followers.

Although Blaise wrote his book mostly to outline history as it related to the Grail Hallows and the church at Glastonbury, those who came after Blaise and Pelagius may have used the manuscript in a later form as a prayer book, or a book around which their teachings revolved. Therefore, it becomes necessary to look to anyone who might have inherited the teachings and the history of the British church at Glastonbury. Since by this time the Roman Church had declared all who followed Pelagius heretics and had excommunicated them, one must exclude Rome and the western empire, which leaves only those who held no trust in, or outwardly disliked, the Roman Church. So it is to the other heretical sects and the Western Empire that this course of research must turn for answers.

Whether modern or medieval, books are finely crafted works of art. From the comic book through romance novels to books of the highest scholarship, each word is there on the page for a reason. Like paintings, books do not contain random, useless features. Instead, each sentence, each brush stroke helps create an end result that would be quite different if that one sentence or brush stroke were omitted.

Much like the Grail hero must ask the right questions, so must the reader of a medieval text or the researcher of a medieval legend wonder about the relevance of every word. To read a text with only passing interest is simply to read an interesting story. However, if one is to learn anything from what is read, careful attention must be paid to what is written. Careful attention to early Grail texts reveals certain themes—stories repeated in each author's version of the manuscript, almost as if these themes had to be present in order to justify calling it a Grail romance.

What purpose do these common themes serve? What ideas are propagated through their inclusion? Most importantly, what historical tidbits were inadvertently included in the story that might be useful to the modern researcher? To find the answers to these questions, these common themes must first be outlined and studied. Obviously certain roles and characters are common to Arthurian tales, but these are all events, characters and ideas that appear to be entities unto themselves embedded in the larger story.

8

Archetypes in
Arthurian Texts

Medieval literature, and especially Arthurian literature, offer certain repeating themes. Among them are the usual themes of brother fighting against brother, son fighting against father, mother manipulating her children, and dramatic death, usually as the result of extraordinary, almost preordained, circumstances. These are the echoes of the classical Greek and Roman traditions of comedy and drama.

When one then ventures into the realms of Arthurian legend and the texts speaking of the Grail Hallows, several other important "distinguishing" features arise. There is the Grail hero, who attains the Grail at last; King Arthur and his knights; a rich cast of enemies to fight; and, of course, the relics themselves, which appear to have a life of their own. However, these are simply "surface features" on the Arthurian landscape. If one knows what to look for, it becomes apparent that almost every word, every event seems to point toward a mystery. Reading the full body of core Arthurian texts allows one to see that several objects, characters, events, and ideas remain ever-present, regardless of the author.

Reflecting on these themes leads the reader to an undeniable feeling that some aspects of the story seem a little out of place, almost like residue from earlier tellings. For example, why is the Grail King wounded? Why must the hero ask about the Grail he sees passing before him? Why does such calamity befall him when he fails to do so? Why is there an endless line of riddles woven throughout? While it is true that a certain degree of "magic" and unrealness is inherent in the genre known as "medieval romance," the Grail texts seem almost overflowing with the unusual.

If a study of the Grail and the Hallows teaches anything, it is that most often things are not what they seem. Therefore, if the story states that three doves appear in the King's chamber window three days in a row—one white, one gray, and one red—the reader immediately picks up on the fact that this is meant to be a portent of things to come. Possibly the king will be visited by the hand of God three times—once bringing the dismal, stormy times indicated by the color gray; once bringing the bloodshed of war indicated by red; and finally, once bringing the peace indicated by the color white. This is, of course, a dramatic oversimplification; however, it demonstrates how small things, repeated and singled out, can hold meaning.

With this in mind, one must visit the Grail texts not only with eyes fully open, but with eyes keen enough to spot the tracks left by earlier traditions pertaining to the Arthurian story. It then becomes possible to fully appreciate the antiquity and complexity of the Grail legend and that of the other Hallows. A good place to begin this study of Arthurian and Grail archetypes is *Sir Gawain and the Green Knight*, and the theme of the beheading knight's challenge.

In this late-fourteenth-century story, Gawain is a member of King Arthur's court taking part in a feast to honor the close of another year. The festivities only serve to irritate the King, who chastises his court, saying that their jaded attitude toward their knightly duties dishonors the court. Hoping to arouse the court's pride, Arthur calls for one show of valor before the year ends.

As fortune and the medieval romancer would have it, such a challenge arrives in the form of a decidedly supernatural-looking knight offering a simple exchange. He calls for one knight to step forward and cleave his head from his neck, the only condition being that, afterward, the Green Knight could return the cut in like manner. Accepting the challenge, Gawain takes the great axe in his hands and strikes the Green Knight's head from his neck. However, the game is far from over. The headless knight strides over to the place where his head came to rest, and returns it to its rightful place. The entire court is aghast and frightened, including Gawain, who can only stand there and face the second part of the challenge.

However, the Green Knight would not have fulfilled his role as the catalyst to ignite sleeping valor if the game had ended so quickly. Instead, he offers Gawain one year in which to prepare himself to face the magical knight again. With this, the Green Knight rides away, leaving Gawain alone with the shadow of certain death looming over him. After his year's time adventuring has passed, Gawain finds himself in the court of the good King Bertilak, who has offered him anything his heart desires—under the condition he repays in like manner what kindness is offered him.

The Queen's love for Gawain soon grows, and with her husband away on a three-day hunting trip, she offers, among other things, three kisses and a sash (as a love token) to her fair knight. Trapped between honoring Bertilak and being honor-bound never to refuse a gift from a lady, Gawain accepts the gifts. Almost immediately, Bertilak returns, asking what comfort his wife has given Gawain in his absence. Gawain straightaway gives Bertilak three kisses—a customary greeting at that time; however, he neglects to return to Bertilak the sash the Queen gave him.

When Gawain goes to meet the Green Knight again, his year being at an end, Gawain kneels for his cut. The Green Knight raises his axe, and Gawain flinches. The Knight chides Gawain for his fear, and begins again; this time Gawain remains still as stone. When the axe falls, Gawain suffers only a scratch. When he arises, he sees that the Green Knight had been Bertilak all along, testing not only this knight's valor, but his honor as well. Bertilak explains that he would have come away from the confrontation with no wound had he but returned the sash. The scratch made by the deadly blade was the only recompense for Gawain's misdeed.

Although this theme varies slightly from text to text, the basic structure of the story remains the same. Sometimes the cut is not a game at all, but repayment for the death of a brother. Sometimes the knight from Arthur's court is not Gawain, but Lancelot or Perceval. The particulars may change, but the main points remain the same—there is a beheading, there is the promise of repayment after one year, and the member of Arthur's court who kneels for the cut always comes away with a minor wound (if any wound at all).

Here one might question what relevance this story has to an investigation of the Grail Hallows. The answer may, in fact, point to one of the relics itself.

The story of the Green Knight tricking a knight from King Arthur's court into playing a game of beheading and death delayed can be likened in several ways to the events that lead to the beheading of John the Baptist. John was beheaded when Herod was tricked into promising the Baptist's head on a platter to his daughter Salome in return for a seductive dance on the occasion of his birthday. Like Gawain, Herod was too quick to play a part in a game that at first seemed safe enough, but soon got out of hand.

The occasion for Herod was not the year's end, as it was for Arthur's court, but the end of another year of his life. Similarly, Herod's opportunity to repay John's death seemed to come some time later as well. After the death of John the Baptist, Herod heard about a fellow by the name of Jesus, whose acts and beliefs sounded very much like that of John. Herod actually believed on some level that Jesus was John the Baptist alive again, sent to make him pay for the beheading. Some time later, when Jesus faced death, it was to the same Herod, Herod Antipas, that Pilate sent Jesus for trial. Although the time between John's death and the crucifixion of Jesus was not one year, the theme of waiting a period of time for one's deeds to come back on oneself remains the same.

It must be noted that, although *Sir Gawain and the Green Knight* is the most popular version of the "beheading knight" story, it is not oldest. A similar story can be found in the thirteenth-century text *Perlesvaus: or the High History of the Holy Grail* in which Lancelot has to face the beheading knight.

> "Sir," saith he to the knight, "What is your pleasure?" "Sir, needs must you cut me off my head with this axe, for of this weapon hath my death been adjudged, but and you will not, I will cut off your own therewith" [*Perlesvaus*, branch VII, title XII].

> With that, he swingeth the axe and cutteth off the head with such a sweep that he maketh it fly seven foot high from the body. The Knight fell to the ground when his head was cut off, and Lancelot flung down the axe, and thinketh that he will make but an ill stay there for himself. He cometh to his horse, and taketh his arms and mounteth and looketh behind him, but seeth neither the body of the Knight nor the head [*Perlesvaus*, branch VII, title XIII].

The cut is later repaid when Lancelot returns to the city in which he had killed the knight.

> Lancelot called to remembrance the knight that he had slain in the Waste City whither behoved him to go, and knew well that the day whereon he should come was drawing nigh [*Perlesvaus*, branch XX, title XII].

> "That shall you know," saith he, "or ever you depart hence. Have you not loyally promised hereof that you would set your head in the same jeopardy as the knight set his, whom you slew without defence? And no otherwise may you depart therefrom. Wherefore now come forward without delay and kneel down and stretch your neck even as my brother did, and so will I smite off your head, and, if you do nor this of your own good will, you shall soon find one that shall make you do it perforce, were you twenty knights as good as you are one. But well I know that you have not come hither for this, but only to fulfil your pledge, and that you will raise no contention herein" [*Perlesvaus*, branch XX, title XIII].

> The knight lifteth up the axe. Lancelot heareth the blow coming, boweth his head and the axe misseth him. He saith to him, "Sir

Knight, so did not my brother that you slew; rather, he held his head and neck quite still, and so behoveth you to do!"

Two damsels appeared at the palace-windows of passing great beauty, and they knew Lancelot well. So, as the knight was aiming a second blow, one of the damsels crieth to him, "And you would have my love for evermore, throw down the axe and cry the knight quit! Otherwise have you lost me for ever!"

The knight forthwith flingeth down the axe and falleth at Lancelot's feet and crieth mercy of him as of the most loyal knight in the world [*Perlesvaus*, branch XX, title XIII].

Lancelot's love for Guinevere and his mourning of her death in the lines prior to the above quote incited the two damsels to come down and save the life of the helpless knight from the sure death he faced.

The story of Lancelot and Guinevere is a legend within a legend. Lancelot has become a symbol of the tragedy that can result from the collision of love and honor. Most medieval scholars believe that the character of Lancelot is most likely an archetypal character rather than an historical one. Although his role in the overarching story is clear, one may wonder why he is portrayed as "the best knight in the world," and has so many other texts devoted to him alone, when he remains hopelessly unable to free himself from the fetters of his adulterous love for his best friend's wife.

In later texts, Lancelot's failure is vindicated by his own son, Galahad. Depicted as almost supernatural in his perfection, Galahad is the only one of Arthur's knights who can sit in the "Seige Perilous"—the seat at Arthur's round table meant to represent the chair once occupied by Judas, who betrayed Jesus at the Last Supper. It was said that no one could sit in the seat without being swallowed up by it or consumed by fire. Clearly, the son of the wayward Lancelot was meant to be the absolute Grail hero, stealing the thunder from the original Grail winner, Perceval.

The conspicuousness of Galahad, and the fact that he only becomes the Grail hero in later manuscripts, would indicate that his character was created as the *perfection* in answer to his father's *imperfection*. To find the perfect knight's creator, one must consider the characteristics that allowed Galahad to become the Grail hero. First, he is described as a "perfect virgin knight." Again we see the idea that only those absolutely devoid of worldly vice, much like Christ Himself, can come near to the Grail. Most previous versions of the Grail story describe Perceval as the "Perfect Fool"— hardly made from the same stuff as Galahad, it would seem.

One must consider that, according to the rules set down by the laws of chivalry and courtly protocol, Lancelot was still acting in accordance with the mandates by which he must live. He both served his king dutifully and honored without question his "Lady Love." It is assumed that Lancelot and Guinevere were lovers; however, the texts for the most part do not explicitly state this. It is only said that Lancelot was cursed with a love for his king's wife. Though undoubtedly this was not a proper kind of love, from the strictest standpoint of chivalric laws he was still within bounds (albeit teetering on the edge).

Therefore, one may assume that someone who felt the "best knight in the world" should be even better created the character of Galahad from Lancelot's line. Since he is described as "perfect" and "virginal," one may correctly assume that Galahad was an embodiment of all things that groups such as the Pelagians and Cathars strove to be. He was strong and fearless, and, most importantly, he existed only to serve God. He shunned entirely what the world offered. If the character of Galahad was added to the Grail tradition, it seems clear that his characteristics reflect a heavy Cathar influence. Galahad was the perfect virgin Knight-Monk, capable of coming closer to God that anyone else, including his father Lancelot and the original Grail Knight, Perceval.

The image of women was not always so lovely as that portrayed in the romantic stories of Lancelot and Guinevere. At times, women were not prizes to be won, but burdens to be borne. Such is the case with the "loathly lady" stories in medieval literature. These were tales typified by a knight, usually caught acting disrespectfully toward women or otherwise conducting themselves in a manner unbecoming a knight, being pressed into marriage with an old, ugly woman, sometimes referred to as a "hag." Examples of this type of story can be found in Chaucer's *Canterbury Tales* (specifically in the "Wife of Bath's Tale"), as well as other manuscripts, such as Marie de France's *Lanval*, and *The Marriage of Sir Gawain and Dame Ragnell*—all of which are set during the Arthurian saga.

However these stories aren't just a medieval answer to feminism. They teach a lesson about courtly behavior and the way a knight should treat a lady. The most clearly defined message in one of these "Old Hag" tales is found in *Lanval*, in which the knight in question is accused of raping a young maiden. After being pressed by the Queen with the quest to find an answer to the riddle, "What does a woman want?" the young knight encounters the Old Hag, who offers to reveal the answer if he promises to marry her. After some arguing and contemplation, the knight agrees.

Finally, when the knight's time to answer the riddle arrives, the old woman offers her knight a choice. She says he can either have a wife that is young and beautiful, but untrustworthy, or she can be old and ugly, but be as good a wife to the knight as ever a woman could be. The knight sees no escape from his predicament, so he offers the choice to the woman herself. Immediately, the woman becomes young and beautiful, but the knight also finds that she will be a good wife to him as well. In offering the choice to the woman, he also answers the Queen's riddle—the woman most wanted "sovereignty," or, in modern terms, "respect." As the knight's reward for his newfound understanding of women, he receives a wife who is both young and beautiful as well as loyal and good.

This image of having to chose between a young, deceptive wife and an old, trustworthy wife parallels the choice that Pelagius had to make between the Roman Church and his British Church. Medieval imagery commonly depicted Christianity as a beautiful young woman with long, flowing blonde hair riding astride a white horse, while depicting Judaism as an Old Hag riding a dragon. In examining the "loathly lady" stories so often seen in Arthurian literature with this unflattering imagery of the Mosaic tradition in mind, it is easy to see that the idea of being rewarded after turning over your fate to the Old Hag would appeal to the Pelagians—in choosing their "old" love, they receive the "new" love of Christ as well.

The description as "the best knight in the world" also seems conspicuous, not as much in terms of Lancelot and Galahad, but because it was also used to describe another notable character in the Grail legend—Joseph of Arimathea. One may simply dismiss this curious wording as a tool used by medieval writers to exemplify, in terms familiar to them at that time, the goodness or holiness of Joseph. However, one cannot think of the image of Joseph as an old man, walking with a staff, carrying the two vials that were the first Grail relics, and in any way describe him as a knight. Who would consider him worthy of the title "knight" without him being a fighting man?

Again one must consider the Cathars and their close associates, the Knights Templar. The Grail knights of the medieval manuscripts are described much like the Knights Templar, with their old, haggard appearance and their white tunics blazoned with a red cross. If the Cathars had some influence on the creation of early Grail manuscripts, surely the knights of Arthur's court would have been much like the Templars, reflecting their piety. For the same reason, Joseph of Arimathea, the "father" of the Grail legend, required a description fitting his role as defender of the relics of Christ's Passion (a title shared by the Templars and Cathars), as well as a holy man worthy of such honor. Where this description was not used for Joseph, a similar one would have been employed, such as "Good Knight" or "Holy Knight."

The term is also used to describe the Grail hero Perceval, who is descended from Joseph's lineage. Turning again to the manuscript *Perlesvaus*, one not only sees Perceval described in these terms, but also how he relates to Joseph of Arimathea.

> Perceval cometh nigh the castle in company with his sister, and knoweth again the chapel that stood upon four columns of marble between the forest and the castle, there where his father told him how much ought he to love good knights, and that none earthly thing might be of greater worth, and how none might know yet who lay in the coffin until such time as the Best Knight of the world should come thither, but that then should it be known. Perceval would fain have passed by the chapel, but the damsel saith to him: "Sir, no knight passeth hereby save he go first to see the coffin within the chapel."
>
> He alighteth and setteth the damsel to the ground, and layeth down his spear and shield and cometh toward the tomb, that was right fair and rich. He set his hand above it. So soon as he came nigh, the sepulchre openeth on one side, so that one saw him that was within the coffin [*Perlesvaus*, branch XV, title XXIII].

The reader later learns that when the coffin opened, all could see that it was Joseph inside, as certified by the relics found within, including the pincers Joseph used to remove the nails from the cross. After Perceval left the coffin, it closed again, and it was written on the coffin that it was Joseph who lay in the crypt.

It would seem that whoever wrote *Perlesvaus* knew of Melkin's writing, which spoke of Joseph's tomb and the fact that relics were to be found inside. Although some details in this passage differ, it demonstrates that the writer knew Joseph's coffin contained relics and had an inscription on the lid. These facts indicate that Melkin's text, or perhaps copies of it, were likely used as source material for the creation of the Grail text.

The last enigmatic, yet ever-present Arthurian character seen lurking in the background of the story may be the most mysterious—and the most telling—of all. Each Grail text mentions the Hallows in one form or another, including the one that seems both the most out of place and the most curious—the sword. In each classical Grail text, a magical sword is seen in close proximity to the Grail Procession.

It is important to remember the identity of this sword in the context of the Grail Hallows—the identity of the sword used to behead John the Baptist, and the only relic not pertaining to Jesus and His crucifixion. One may wonder why this relic, associated with another, albeit closely related, biblical character, is included with this very special cache of Christian relics.

The sword is no less mysterious in the texts themselves. Although the Grail, the Lance, and often a second vessel is carried into the hall of the Fisher King amid resplendent light and beauty by fair maidens or young pages, the sword is excluded from the traditional procession. Instead, it is introduced either just before or just after the other Hallows. Only in the Grail text *La Folie Perceval* is the sword seen alongside the other relics. Although not officially part of this otherworldly procession, the sword remains as magical as the other relics.

To demonstrate the unusual characteristics of this object, one need only compare two of the texts that claim to come from the same source, but which differ greatly, both in style and focus. Consider the accounts of the Grail Procession as detailed in Chretien de Troyes' *Le Conte del Graal* and Wolfram von Eschenbach's *Parzival*. For purposes of comparison, a compressed version of both accounts, including the appearance of the magical sword, appear below—Chretien first, followed by Eschenbach.

> While they thus talked, a young attendant entered at the door, a sword hanging by the rings from his neck. He handed it to the wealthy man. The latter, drawing it out halfway, clearly saw where it had been made, this being engraved on the blade. He also noticed that it was made of such fine steel that it could not break into pieces except by a singular peril known only to the man who had forged it.
>
> While they talked of this and that, a young attendant entered the room, holding a shining lance by the middle of its shaft. He passed between the fire and those seated on the bed, and all present saw the shining lance with its shining head. A drop of blood fell from the tip of the lance, and that crimson drop ran all the way down to the attendant's hand.
>
> Two more attendants then entered, bearing in their hands candelabra of fine gold inlaid with niello. Handsome indeed were the attendants carrying the candelabra. On each candelabrum then candles, at the very least, were burning. Accompanying the attendants was a beautiful, gracious, and elegantly attired young lady holding between her two hands a bowl. When she entered holding this serving bowl, such brilliant illumination appeared that the candles lost their brightness just as the stars and the moon do with the appearance of the sun. Following her was another young lady holding a silver carving platter. The bowl, which came first, was of fine pure gold, adorned with many kinds of precious jewels, the richest and most costly found on sea or land, those on the bowl undoubtedly more valuable than any others [Chretien de Troyes].

> A squire came quickly through the door
> And a lance with iron point he bore
> (A rite that caused them bitter woe)
> Which dripped with blood in steady flow,
> Then down the shaft into the hand;
> The sleeve its further progress banned.
> All those assembled wept and cried
> Throughout the spacious hall and wide.

Maidens were they pure and fair
With garlands laid upon their hair.
Their coiffure was of flowers.
On the hand of each there towers
Of gold a handsome candlestick.
Their curls were long, blonde, and thick.
They carried candles burning.

Four carried candles great and tall,
The others did not mind at all
To bear a precious stone and fine
Through which by day the sun could shine.
This gave the name by which 'twas known:
A garnet-hyacinth. The stone
Was amply wide and amply long,
Cut thin, for lightness' sake, but strong,
To make a table of it.

After them appeared the queen.
So bright the maiden's face and mien,
All thought the down was breaking.
The clothes her raiment making
Were costly silks of Araby.
Upon a deep green Achmardi
She bore the pride of Paradise,
Root and branch, beyond all price.
That was a thing men call the Grail,
Which makes all earthly glory pale.

Bearing a sword whose sheath alone
'Twould cost a thousand marks to own.
While thus he thought, a squire drew near,
Its hilt was of one ruby made
And then it seemed as if the blade
Were a source of many wonders blest.
The host bestowed in on the guest
    [Wolfram von Eschenbach].

In both versions of the Procession account, a magical sword is given
to the Grail hero, Perceval, by the Fisher King, who later turns out to be
Perceval's uncle, making Perceval the rightful heir to, and finder of, the
Grail and its Hallows. In Chretien's tale, the sword arrives first, indeed
immediately before the Procession. In Wolfram's story, which he claims comes
from the same sourcebook, the sword arrives *immediately after* the Procession. It is later stated that this sword, once owned by the Fisher King himself, will never break—with one exception. Some texts indicate that it will
fail its bearer at the moment of his most dire need. In other texts, including

both Chretien's version and Wolfram's, the sword will only fail in a specific situation known solely to he who forged it. However, in all cases, it seems the sword can be repaired by magical means. Not only is this sword that breaks only under special circumstances a common feature in the Grail texts, a broken sword can also be seen in a Cathar "cave of initiation" found in Southern France near the Pyrenees.

If these were the only places this image occurred, it would simply stand as an intriguing mystery. However, a broken sword is found in two other places that would indicate connections to the legend of the Grail Hallows. A relic resembling a broken sword joined together by an inscribed golden collar rests in the Hapsburg Museum in Vienna, Austria. (Throughout history, this object has been thought to be the Spear of Destiny or the Lance of Longinus.) And the sword appears in yet another unforeseen place—the Tarot deck. Besides the fact that the sword is one of the four suits of the Minor Arcana, a broken sword blade in the Devil's hand on the "Devil" card from the Major Arcana.

With the sword found throughout the Grail legend—and all over medieval Europe—is it simply coincidence that the sword is said to be broken while a relic called the Sword of St. Maurice now sits in two halves in an Austrian museum? The sword is possibly the most puzzling of all the Hallows. However, its uniqueness and mystery may provide important historical information that may well open the book that tells the story of the Grail Hallows' history.

9

Eschenbach's *Parzival* and the Fisher King

It would appear that many Arthurian and Grail legends can be identified by certain repeating themes. Although much of classical literature is built on a foundation of heroic archetypes and common topics, the characters and events found throughout this very specific type of medieval literature seem to go beyond a simple literary tool. They almost present the appearance of familiar landmarks left behind in different people's description of the same place, perhaps to indicate that the reader is following a set path.

Although these themes are common enough to be conspicuous, some are conspicuous enough to warrant close investigation. The different versions of these texts may shuffle around these commonalities or couch them in vague reference, but all of the Grail romancers agree that some things must remain constant. Some themes must be left untouched in a true Grail text. As has been demonstrated, the early texts consider the Grail to be on the same level as the other relics of the procession known as the Grail Hallows. And second only to these relics is their curious guardian—the enigmatic king, mortally wounded without dying, known as the Fisher King.

In studying the legends of the Grail and the Hallows, the reader is introduced to many strange characters who seem to possess some meaning beyond that which is readily apparent—knights who ride their horses facing backwards, beautiful maidens in tattered clothing, and monks living deep in the woods wearing rusted chain mail shirts, to name only a few. But of all the characters the reader—or, in fact, the Grail hero himself—encounters, none is more important than the Fisher King.

The Fisher King, or King Fisherman, is the oldest of all the characters involved with the legend. He is inextricably linked to Grail history and its story—the ancientness of his role rivaling that of Joseph himself. And the character of the Fisher King is of vital importance in understanding the mysteries surrounding the Grail Hallows. As mysteriously as the quest ending with a question, the Fisher King's pain holds his realm in the misery of its own half-death.

In the traditional body of the Grail texts, the Grail hero Perceval first sees the Fisher King fishing in the waters surrounding his castle, or else in waters near enough to his castle to be seen by Perceval while speaking to the Fisher King. Perceval asks the fisherman where he may shelter along his wearying journey, and the fisherman tells him the way to the only castle nearby, which the reader later learns belongs to the fisherman himself.

When Perceval reaches the gates, he says that a fisherman told him to come to that place for shelter, and on these words alone the knight is welcomed into the castle and into the banquet hall, where he receives rich clothing and every comfort he desires. After being made welcome, Perceval is again introduced to the fisherman who bade him come to this place, only now it becomes clear to him that the fisherman was no simple angler, but the king of the castle.

At this stage of the story the Grail procession is about to begin. However, it is also the point at which another important event takes place. As Perceval luxuriates in the Fisher King's hospitality, he notices the company in which he finds himself. Although some texts mention the others present as simply honorable knights (if it mentions them at all), their description in the German text *Parzival*, by Wolfram von Eschenbach, is very close in appearance to members of the Knights Templar.

Another event of importance occurs at this point. Chretien's text (differing from Eschebach's) states that just before the procession begins, the Fisher King gives Perceval the magical sword that will never break— with one, and only one, exception. In Eschenbach's version the Fisher King presents the sword just following the Grail procession, but it's clear it is the same sword. It would almost appear that the sword is given to the Grail hero as a *second prize*, either because he has just failed to ask the important question, or because the Fisher King knows of the hero's weakness, and so gives him the sword instead of the Grail Hallows' guardianship.

Another interesting aspect of the Fisher King's feast has to do with the beginning of the procession itself. While both versions of the tale have in common the theme that the achievement of the Grail will heal the wound, and thereby the king, they vary in focus. While the Grail is at the center of the procession in Chretien's text, leading to jubilation among those present at the feast, Eschenbach's account of the procession concentrates on the lance, and the mourning the attendants of the feast experience when the lance enters the banquet hall.

The friction between not only Chretien and Eschenbach, but between the alleged validity of their retelling of the sourcebook, is famous among medievalists familiar with Grail literature. While it was not uncommon for medieval writers to claim their work was a more faithful retelling of the story in question than another writer's version, the marked difference in tone between the two texts seems to indicate something more than mere literary rivalry. While Chretien wrote the familiar story of courtly love, questing, and virginal honor, Eschenbach wrote a much darker tale, dealing with the love (and sometimes distaste) of women, abandonment of— and by—God, and the role of the supernatural aspects of the Grail (his account speaking of a jewel that fell from Lucifer's crown as he tumbled to earth from Heaven).

These differences could be dismissed if it were not for one simple fact. Chretien's version of the Grail story is incomplete, whereas Eschenbach's version comes to a resolution. If his claim that he used the same sourcebook as Chretien is to be believed, Eschenbach's final five chapters came from a part of the sourcebook missing from Chretien's tale. Although many would argue that he simply extrapolated on Chretien's text, as has been said of Chretien's "continuators," one must at least consider the possibility that Eschenbach's final five chapters speak to a lost portion of the Grail saga.

Although it is impossible to know for sure if Eschenbach truly based his account on the same sourcebook as did Chretien de Troyes, his mention of Kyot as the provider of the sourcebook, and of a "heathen" named Flegatanis as its author, does suggest that he had at least some familiarity with the sourcebook. The name Kyot can be traced back to Toledo Spain and the possibility that the tale emerged from the mists of legend as the result of a fortuitous literary meeting of the minds, bringing texts from fringe lands to noble European courts.

Wolfram von Eschenbach's *Parzival* is an interesting study in the Grail Hallows mysteries for a number of reasons. Although it claims the same heritage as Chretien's French text, it is vastly different. It is a more esoteric, magical treatment of the legend, and has a much more visceral feel. Also, it focuses more on the lance than the Grail, and does so with a tone of lamentation. Finally, and most intriguingly, it more thoroughly covers the Fisher King and his own history with the relics than does Chretien's account. It is because of this curious change in focus that this text becomes important to a study of the Grail Hallows. Its focus on both the lance and the wounded Grail King may serve to answer questions not dealt with as clearly in its French counterpart.

The story of the Fisher King is one of devastation, anguish, and the curse of living. According to tradition, the Fisher King was the last Grail guardian before the arrival of the Grail hero Perceval. He is also called the "Maimed King," due to an injury that befell him known as the "Dolorous Blow." Usually little is said about how the king became so injured, with texts offering only a vague explanation that the wound resulted from some unnamed sin committed by the Fisher King, either a loss of faith or lust. The only clear account of this wound's origin is found in Eschenbach's text.

He posits that the wound was inflicted during a jousting match. What caused the wound to fester and refuse to heal, however, is the *reason* the king participated in the joust. He broke the one vow a protector of the Grail Hallows must adhere to—that he remain pure, devoid of any and all lust for women. The Fisher King broke that vow when he participated in the match in honor of a woman. Therefore, his wounding in the genitals became a clear indication that his ceaseless suffering was a result of him putting his love for a woman above his love for God and His Grail.

Although the lance in this case is a simple jousting lance, its inclusion with the Grail and other Hallows of the procession makes it clear that the spear is still meant to represent the Lance of Longinus—the lance that pierced Christ's side. Just as the wound itself was a holy judgment on the Fisher King's indiscretion, the instrument of the wound, the spear, was an allegorical reference to God's holy lance. It is here that one must stop to make a vitally important consideration. If the lance is representative of sin, and the wound representative of God's judgment, might the character of the Fisher King be a representation of something more symbolic? Although the goal of this investigation of the Grail Hallows is to dispel the myth that the legend is *only* a symbolic tale, one must understand that there is a great deal of symbolism and representation found in the Grail texts.

In some versions of the story, the Fisher King is said to be only one or two generations removed from Joseph of Arimathea. Indeed, one text mentions the Fisher King's name as Bron. Since some accounts of Joseph arriving at Wearyall hill include a member amongst his company named Bron, this would seem to indicate that he was contemporaneous with Joseph himself. Since most would agree that a man, outside of the stories from the Bible, cannot live from the time of Joseph in the first century to the time of Arthur in the sixth century, it is likely that this figure of such great importance to the Grail legend is a character meant to represent an idea rather than a person. For this reason, it becomes necessary to delve into the character of the Fisher King to see what he was created to represent.

The most important part of the Fisher King character is his link to the state of his kingdom. In sinning, he is cursed to linger between life and death, plagued by constant pain. Kept alive only by the Grail's healing power of sacredness, the king, in a sense, remains alive as a punishment. In some texts, the king dies after his curse is lifted and the question is asked about the Grail. However, as king, he doesn't suffer alone.

Called the "Wasteland Kingdom," the king's land is doomed to suffer until his wound heals. Although one might think this a clear indication of Celtic influence on the Grail legend, the king's life does not seem to dictate the fate of his land as much as does his redemption. Even if the king dies, his kingdom regains its prosperity when the Grail is achieved. Although most kingdoms of the time relied on the king for its own prosperity, this is not just a simple case of a king neglecting his lands. This is an entire population forced to pay the price for one person's failure. This fact begs the question: if the Fisher King is a symbolic character, what is represented by his cursed kingdom?

Consider the overall picture of the Fisher King and his doomed lands. Here is an image of one man who makes a mistake he knew he should not make, and the people under his care are made to suffer for it. It is the classic sheep and shepherd story on a grand and mythical scale. A similar story of sheep and shepherds comes from the Bible, which describes both Jesus and his disciples as being the shepherds of lost sheep. In a sense, the story of the Fisher King becomes a story of a poor disciple.

A similar comparison can help shed some light on the character of the Fisher King. In the early days of the Christian faith, the symbol of the fish became the emblem of the early church. The disciples were also called "fishers of men," meaning that they would gather mankind to them and thereby to Jesus' teaching. Therefore, the "King Fisherman" may be a symbol for one who tries to emulate Jesus and become the king of all "fishers of men"—a man fishing alone in the great waters of the wilderness.

If the Fisher King is the symbol of one who tried and failed to become the perfect disciple, and his kingdom symbolizes the lost sheep he failed to serve, what can be inferred by the method in which the king is healed and the kingdom restored? To achieve the Grail and to redeem the king, Perceval must ask a question of the Fisher King. In Chretien's text, the question that must be asked is: What is the Grail and who is served by it? However, Wolfram von Eschenbach makes the question much closer to the king himself. In his version of the story, Parzival must ask King Anfortas: "Uncle, what is it that troubles you?"

The asking of this question reminds the Fisher King of what is important, of his responsibility, and to whom he owes his own allegiance. When he "repents" of his sin, he is returned to a state of perfection and purity, once again worthy of serving the Grail—and perhaps reaching the end of his life as a reward for his years of great suffering. Therefore, one may take this to mean that if one is to become worthy of the Grail, of God's grace, and able to lead other men into righteousness, he must first question. However, one must then figuratively answer a question with a question: What must be questioned? To grasp this, the Fisher King must be understood in the context of the Grail Hallows' history. This again leads back to the Isle of Avalon and the sacred ground of Glastonbury.

The name given to the Fisher King by Robert de Boron is "Bron," very similar to Bran the Blessed of Celtic mythology, but also said to be one of Joseph's company at Glastonbury. However, most other texts give him names such as Pelles, or Pellam, and go on to say that he is the uncle of the Grail hero Perceval. If one takes into consideration the facts that the Fisher King is most commonly named something sounding like "Pelles," and that the character seems to come from a time close to the foundation of the legend itself and contemporary with the Arthurian period, it seems quite reasonable to think that the character of the Fisher King, Pelles, was based on the historical figure of Pelagius.

Although this may at first seem too great a leap of faith to hazard, if one remembers the symbolic characteristics of the Fisher King, as well as what he is meant to represent, Pelagius appears to fit the description very well. The Fisher King was the guardian of the Holy Grail and the Hallows, not to mention the lord over a great court. He was, in a way, a shepherd over his flock of followers. In the same manner, Pelagius was a guardian of the Grail tradition at Glastonbury, where an entire colony of devotees placed their fate, in a sense, in his hands when he ventured to Rome to stand before the great and powerful Roman Church.

As one who saw himself as a fisher of men, Pelagius went to do spiritual and theological battle with the Roman Papacy, armed with the well-known tradition of relics housed at Glastonbury. Then, when he failed to gain the approval of the Church, he may have felt he failed the church of Britain. When he and his theology was subsequently declared heretical, resulting in the excommunication of himself and all of his followers, he or those who later wrote of him may have seen his failure as a sin of pride that damned them all.

The history of the Pelagian heresy in Britain is a true-to-life retelling of the Fisher King legend. The Grail "king" or chief defender went into battle, seeking a fate beyond simple meditation in God's service, and was wounded by the Roman Church, possibly with their claim that they too held a sacred relic of the Crucifixion—the lance. His failure resulted in the whole community's permanent separation from God in the form of a mass excommunication, thus making their once joyous tradition at Glastonbury into one of a spiritually miserable and melancholy wasteland.

However, his eventful visit to Rome is not the only reason to believe the character of the Fisher King is based on Pelagius and his movement. First, the Fisher King was said to be a Grail guardian, and one only a few generations distant from Joseph of Arimathea. Pelagius did indeed live only about 350 years after Joseph, and was clearly a part of the Grail tradition at Glastonbury.

Second, if his "Grail Castle" is thought of in more general terms, the "castle" could be the place in Britain where the Grail relics were held— Glastonbury Abbey. In fact, this would be in keeping with the previous discussion of the blurred use of medieval, kingly and knightly terminology to describe things of great holiness. In other words, if Joseph is described as a "holy knight," the church at Glastonbury would be considered his "castle."

Furthermore, Perceval first sees the Fisher King in a boat, fishing in the waters that surround his castle. If one draws a parallel between the church at Glastonbury and the Grail Castle, the landscape between Wearyall Hill and Glastonbury Tor during this time would match perfectly. It must be remembered that the Glastonbury of Pelagius' time was quite different than that which the modern tourist might see upon visiting the abbey. The whole area during that time, well past the time of Arthur, was swampland, with the dry island of the Tor and the abbey grounds surrounded by water, thus creating the mythical "Isle of Avalon."

To make the character of the Fisher King match the historical man Pelagius, several key issues must be resolved. Why was the Fisher King said to linger between life and death? Why was his wound thought to have been caused by the Lance of Longinus? Why is the Grail achieved and the Fisher King released from torment by asking questions instead of finding answers? To answer these questions, one need only look to what was happening with the British church during this time period.

Beginning in the year 380, Pelagius left for Rome with the assertion that he and his followers were the true inheritors of Christ's church because their order was founded by Joseph of Arimathea and possessed the holy relics he brought to Britain. Assuming Pelagius returned to his home in Britain, he came back as quite a different man than the one who had left. Having been excommunicated and turned away from the full European body of Christianity, he would have surely felt lost and abandoned, possibly even by God.

If the Lance of Longinus is representative of God's judgment, the Dolorous Blow and the Fisher King's wound would translate into the Roman church using their possession of the lance and other relics as their weapon against the claims of Pelagius and the British church, destroying his argument—and potentially his motivation—that they should be recognized as another branch of the Christian church. Furthermore, when the Roman Church excommunicated the entire group, his wound was shared by them all. The spiritual effect of this action becomes evident when one considers that the Fisher King's wound is said to have been in the "thigh," which some have interpreted as "loins" or "genitals"—in essence, destroying his potency. Similarly, the disdain of the Roman church would have destroyed the very reason Pelagius felt the church at Glastonbury was so important.

If he returned to Glastonbury with this feeling of abandonment and defeat, having lost the reason to believe in the sacredness of the church there, the community may well have fallen to ruin, its members turning away from their zealous life centered on the church. This idea is reflected in the Somerset story of St. Patrick's visit to Britain and the church at Glastonbury, in which Patrick arrived there to find the wattle church in a state of disrepair. However, it is not to be forgotten that another event of great importance to the Glastonbury church occurred around this time as well. When the Marian Chalice arrived, having been sent there from Rome, around A.D. 410, it must have revived the broken spirits and sagging morale of those still clinging to the remains of the church founded upon the relics brought there by Joseph centuries earlier.

Here it appears that the saga of the Fisher King and the Grail itself plays out in a relatively short period of time, a time close to that of King Arthur and Merlin, culminating in renewed interest in the Grail Hallows and the creation of the first Grail text, written by Blaise. The Olde Chirche played the role of the Grail castle; the Fisher King, Pelles (Pelagius), was wounded when the Lance was spiritually used against him by the Roman church, and the wasteland that such a devastating blow created was redeemed when the Marian Chalice, a Grail cup, was given to the holy order that lived there at Glastonbury.

One question remains. If the Grail is attained by the act of asking a question, what does the wounded Fisher King wish for those who followed him to ask? The key to the importance of the Grail Hallows is located in this question, or, more precisely, in the act of questioning itself. For the Fisher King "Pelles" to be fully redeemed, he not only had to receive the apparent approval of God (in the arrival of the Marian Chalice), he needed again to become worthy of the Grail—to maintain and to guard the legacy of the Grail at Glastonbury. To accomplish this, he had to make known the truth of the Glastonbury church, and the power of the relics that it held. To be a good shepherd again, he needed to find other lost sheep who were at that time not present in his fold. He needed to leave a "path" of sorts for any lost individuals who might wander across it, looking for the right way. Therefore, Pelagius continued the work for which he had gone to Rome, only now he did so with a new focus—to *question* was to find redemption.

Several "heretical" groups shared this sentiment throughout the Middle Ages; but only one group truly stands out. The group who inherited the belief system (as well as, apparently, some of the early writings about the Grail Hallows and their history) was none other than the Cathars, a group who claimed to possess the Holy Grail itself. One may still wonder how much of an influence they had on the development of the Grail legend, and what kind of proof exists to substantiate such claims. It will soon become quite clear that the Grail Hallows were of the utmost importance in the Cathars' culture and practices.

10

Cathar and
Templar Heresies

Beginning an investigation into the historical aspects of the Holy Grail, the Grail Hallows, or any other legend is not something to be undertaken frivolously. Doing so is like walking into a forest of birch trees where the canopy is so full it obscures the sky, creating only meager light. The interplay of light and dark amid the stark, white trunks, themselves looking like old, bleached bones, might give the impression of an evil place, at once both real and surreal, even though it is, in truth, a place rich with life and beauty. The unknown or unfamiliar plays on human fears, causing a heightened sense of alertness. Choosing to walk among our fears, in the hope of finding the light of wisdom, requires one to tread with a gentle step, but also with the courage to expose oneself to that which is feared.

Given the very nature of the legends in question, those trying to find a thread of truth in such stories must walk a very fine line between that light and darkness. It is necessary to mix the most sacred traditions of Christianity with traditions, histories, and objects that have come to be considered "heretical" or "occult." This is not to say that one must blend these traditions, as has become the pattern with the "New Age" movement, but rather that, to fully understand history in a scientific sense, one must for a time suspend what is feared and see it purely in an historical light.

The Dark Ages and Middle Ages can be characterized as times of fear. People feared for their lives, due both to the advance of marauding invaders and to the looming cloud of pestilence and disease. Later, when life no longer hung in the balance to such an extent, church officials kept all in check by describing the fearful things that awaited someone who looked outside the bounds outlined by those same officials. They used the Bible as a weapon of fear, skipping over the message of joy and redemption in order to establish guidelines by which man was to live, and to define Western Civilization's culture in the face of what was considered a barbaric, heathen world.

Therefore, to step outside those bounds was not only looked upon as an unacceptable infraction, but as a danger to the rest of the civilized world—a danger best dealt with as would a fearful gardener encountering a snake among his rows. The danger had to be cut off. Although the Roman Catholic Church of medieval Europe was responsible for some of the most important literature, artwork, and architecture of its time, it was also responsible for travesties inconceivable by the modern mind.

However, just as the Church's fear at the time blinded it to the larger picture, the modern researcher must not be blinded by the negative, and thus fail to see their point of view or the importance of the history for which the Roman Catholic Church as an institution is responsible. In trying to understand the importance of light and dark, or good and evil, at the time, and its role in the development of the Grail Hallows legend, one can find no better example than the Cathar movement in Southern France.

The Cathar were a group of people who, though not necessarily monks in the strictest sense, practiced a monastic life in which their goal was to achieve a state of near-perfection, using Jesus as the yardstick. To call one group of people "Cathars," as has been done with the sect found in France during the Middle Ages, is somewhat of a misnomer. Catharism was an idea shaped by many forces, all of which aligned themselves squarely against many of the main edicts set down by the Roman Catholic Church.

Although Catharism was not considered a formally organized movement until the early eleventh century, the ideas that formed the basis of their doctrine came from a much earlier time.

> There are striking likenesses between Eastern Bogomilism and Western Catharism, especially in their ritual practices and their attitudes towards the beliefs, order and ritual of the great Churches against which they struggled and protested. Both movements restricted prayer to the paternoster alone, repeated in swathes by their respective elites, on lines reminiscent of monastic prayer and with similar frequency [The Cathars, Malcolm Lambert, p. 29].

> Both Bogomils and Cathars rejected the veneration of the cross on comparable quasi-rational grounds, that it was inconceivable that the piece of wood on which his son was killed would be dear to the king. Both gave an allegorical interpretation of the words of Christ instituting the Eucharist. They were alike in having the same weekly fast days,

Mondays, Wednesdays, and Fridays. Both rejected marriage *per se* as a dirty business which perpetuated the reign of Satan, and believed that salvation was only possible when the marriage partners repudiated each other. Both laid great emphasis on the initiation rite, a baptism of the Spirit or of fire, in contrast to the Satanic baptism in water [Lambert, pp. 29–30].

Bogomilism originated in Bulgaria in the tenth century in answer to the practices of the Byzantine Orthodox church, which was seen by them as corrupt and the "Church of Satan." If Bogomilism can be considered an early forerunner of Catharism, the origins of both movements can then be traced back to the beginnings of the larger movement, called "dualism," of which they were both a part.

Dualism got its start in Armenia in the middle of the seventh century when Constantine of Mananalis set forth the idea that there were two Gods—one good God who made man's soul, and one bad God who made man's flesh, "imprisoning" him on the earth. The doctrine of the flesh being an evil prison in which the sacred soul was trapped became the basis of the Cathar belief structure. Toward this end, the Cathars endeavored to make their inherently evil flesh more holy to match their souls, in essence preventing their bodies from dragging their souls into perdition.

Along with this notion of denying the earthly world, Cathars took vows of poverty, celibacy, and devotion to those things that would bring them closer to God. For this reason, they took issue with the practice of worshipping icons and other physical objects of veneration. They also believed that man could achieve closeness to Christ by living a pure life, thus achieving a state of spiritual perfection. This method of attaining "Christ-likeness" through a clean life of poverty and celibacy was not unique. In fact, a similar doctrine had been espoused 200 years before the birth of "duality" by the British monk Pelagius. Today, many scholars and historians theorize that the Pelagian heresy of the fifth century strongly influenced the theological melting pot that became the Cathar movement.

It is easy to see how Pelagianism and other "heretical" movements might have served to corroborate the Cathar belief system. However, several key differences between the two belief systems at first seem to make them polar opposites. For example, the Pelagian church based its claim to be the inheritors of the Christian tradition on their possession of relics of Christ's crucifixion, whereas the Cathars appeared to deplore relics. Pelagius claimed the Old Testament was as good a reference on how to live a virtuous life as the New Testament, while the Cathars believed the Old Testament to be the work of the Devil. Other than their similarity in the belief that perfection could be achieved through clean living, how could it be possible that Pelagianism influenced Catharism?

Several nuances of Cathar beliefs might have caused Pelagius and his followers to be viewed in a somewhat more amiable light. Although the Bogomils abhorred any form of relics, the Cathars did take part in Saint worship, which included relics of the Saints themselves. Further, Cathars drank wine, except on a few holy days of note, whereas the Bogomils rejected wine completely. Also unlike the Bogomils, the Cathars depised anthropomorphic images of God as an old man, Jesus as a bearded adult, and the Holy Ghost as a youth—presumably due to the use of the flesh as symbolism for the sacred (Lambert, p. 33). Ultimately, whatever the origins of the Cathar movement might have been, they must be defined as their own culture.

> The evidence is that, though Catharism was intimately linked with and owed much to the Bogomils and their teachings, it none the less emerged as an independent movement with characteristics of its own and, by the time it was detected by Church authorities, had been thoroughly westernized [Lambert, p. 34].

Whatever other evidence might support the idea that the Cathars of the Middle Ages were influenced by the much earlier Pelagian movement, the clearest indication of the Cathars' familiarity with and closeness to the theology of the Pelagians from the fifth century is the tradition that both held and valued the Holy Grail. While the Pelagians claimed their church was founded on the Joseph of Armiathea tradition in Britain, the Cathars were said to possess the same relic—even going so far as to "slip away" with it during the night before their last stronghold at Montsegur fell to the Pope's forces.

For this reason, if for no other, it would seem the Cathars grew from the Pelagian tradition. However, one may wonder how the relics that founded the first Christian Church in Britain made their way to the Cathars of Southern France almost a millennium later. It appears the answer came on the back of a horse. With the Christianization of Europe, relics spread far and wide along with the word of God. With Rome as the main seaport on the waters of the medieval world, and Constantinople as the gateway to the middle east, Christian relics quickly found their way to far-off places like Africa and Spain. They were both dispersed and collected to a large extent by the same group of people—the Knights Templar.

During the time of the Middle Ages called the Crusades, wealthy Europeans traveled eastward toward the Holy Land with the intention of freeing it from Muslim invaders. While these epic chapters of history have been called everything from a direct mandate from God to a ruthless tram-pling of innocents in the name of wealth and gain, the one thing most agree upon is that they were dangerous times. The ever-present shadow of illness, starvation, and attack made the march east less of a genteel picnic, and more of a nightmare that grew worse with every passing year. Out of this time came many symbols upon which the beaten travelers could place their hopes. Relics were found, and gauged as divine omens indicating the crusaders' eventual success. Many mystic visions came and went, with vary-ing ends. Lastly, a brotherhood was formed. This group of knights were to serve not only as the protectors of their fellow crusaders, but also as their moral compass.

The Knights Templar served as police force, bankers, and the ideal toward which the rest of the legions might aspire. Seen riding two to a horse (symbolizing their frugality and humility, as well as their close kinship to each other), they became a force to be reckoned with by the very church body from which they were created. Soon their power rivaled that of the Church itself, which, needless to say, could not be tolerated.

After some time, the Templars fell from favor and were disbanded—accused of everything from rampant homosexuality to devil worship. Indeed, many were burned at the stake when they refused to admit to such charges. However, from the Templar tradition of the Middle Ages comes a long tradition of relic keeping, as well as ancient knowledge being pro-tected by their scholars. Thus, it's no surprise that the picture of the Grail Knights painted by many early Grail texts look much like the image of a Templar—wearing armor under a white tunic with a red cross blazoned upon it, perhaps obscured slightly by a long white beard (indicating age and wisdom).

Different sources associate several relics and other sacred items as being in the Templars' possession at some point, including the Ark of the Covenant, the candelabra from the Temple of Solomon, ancient early Chris-tian writings not known to the rest of the world (perhaps even the written words of Jesus Himself), Jesus' burial cloth (now known as the Shroud of Turin), the Lance of Longinus, and, lastly, the Holy Grail. Roslyn Chapel in Scotland, a place of safety for what remained of the Templar order after it was forcibly disbanded, is claimed to have once been the resting place for a portion of the True Cross, taken there for protection by the Knights Templar.

It may seem curious that a group of knights that would later be labeled heretics were once trusted guardians of sacred Judeo-Christian relics, but one need only to look into their past to discover why this role was handed to them. While in Jerusalem and other parts of the Holy Land, the Knights

Templar began a campaign of settlement and investigation that lead to a pervasive presence throughout the region, a presence visible even today. Sometimes the Templars would use the very stones from which ancient structures were built to make their own buildings.

Considering this, it may appear that the Knights Templar came to the Holy Land not to protect it, but to use it for their own purposes. However, as is the case with most analyses of historical events, such things are difficult to judge using modern sensibilities. It must be remembered that in these dangerous times survival and preservation were paramount, not multiculturalism. However, even then, the first light of modern archeology shone through. The Knights Templar allegedly excavated the area of the Temple Mount for nine years, eventually finding the maze of tunnels once used by the priests of the original Temple to hide its wealth. It is thought that the Templars found a horde of silver and gold, with which they gained their power and built many of their castles and strongholds.

It is also thought that they found something other than treasure under the Temple Mount. Some postulate that the real reason the Templars fell from grace with the Roman Church is that they discovered scrolls from the first Christian Church in Jerusalem, scrolls that outlined a plan for the continuation of the Christian church much different from that set down by the Roman Catholic Church. Some say that this is why the order was treated with such disdain, and why what remained of the order went underground, surviving in the form of what we now call Freemasonry. Due to their years digging into the ancient past of Judaism and Christianity, the Templars gained a reputation for being "relic hunters" of sorts—a group of people who both found and protected sacred items from the Bible's history. But it was not this practice alone that earned them this reputation. Time spent in another of Europe's centers for relic worship would cement their image.

Constantinople was seen as the "Fort Knox" for Christian relics. It was said that, "...Constantinople was held by the Crusaders to possess more holy relics than the rest of the Christian world" (*The Sword and the Grail*, Andrew Sinclair, p. 74). One must remember that Constantinople was built by its namesake, Emperor Constantine, whose mother, Helena Augusta, is said to have found Christ's tomb and the many relics therein. The boundaries of the city were allegedly drawn out by Constantine with a spear head in which he had embedded a nail from the cross of the Crucifixion. Therefore, it should come as no surprise that this city, above all others in Europe at the time, would be the one place where relics might congregate.

Another possible contributing factor to why Constantinople (present day Istanbul, Turkey) was such a center for holy items is that the city nearly became the new Rome during an early schism between eastern and western Europe. Consequently, the Byzantine Emperors sought to collect holy relics, such as the True Cross (or at least pieces of it), the Lance of Longinus (and all of its competing lances from around Europe), and the Shroud of Turin (found there during the first Crusade by none other than the Knights Templar). With their time spent digging in the ancient soil of Jerusalem, as well as rummaging through the relic storehouses of Constantinople, it is clear why the Templars were seen as the keepers of the Grail Hallows. If any Christian body possessed these relics, who else but the Templars could have it?

One may see why the Templars were thought to have relics such as the Grail Hallows among their treasures, but what connection did they have with the Cathars? The Templars were "warrior monks" possessing wealth and power, while the Cathars were religious idealists who shunned the earthly world and all of its pursuits and pleasures. However, both groups advocated celibacy, took a vow of poverty (at least to be poor individually), and ultimately were labeled as heretics by the Pope. Reading the accusations made against both parties, it sounds almost as if they were one and the same. In fact, there does appear to have been some shared sympathy between the two during the time of their mutual tribulation.

> Another missing link between Cathars and the Grail is provided by the Templars who, historically, refused to crusade against the first and, according to Wolfram, were the guardians of the second. They had a major commandery at Capoulet-Junac between Tarascon and Montreal-de-Sos [*In Search of the Holy Grail and the Precious Blood*, Ean and Deike Begg, p. 57].

It is impossible to say whether the Cathars' alliance with the Templars prompted the common belief that the Cathars possessed relics of Christ's Passion. However, the idea was so strong that, after the Cathar stronghold at Montsegur fell, the Pope ordered his forces to search the ruins for any such holy relics as they might find (they found none). Tradition states that four brothers of the order fled Montsegur during the night with the Grail to prevent its capture. It is possible that they took it to their somewhat more resourceful contemporaries, the Knights Templar.

The Crusade against the Cathars in which the Templars refused to take part is known as the Albeginsian Crusade—the systematic execution, ordered by Pope Innocent III in 1243, of men, women, and children who were sympathetic to the Cathar cause. Montsegur, the last Cathar fortress to fall in this Crusade, has become famous not for its role in the Grail legend, but because it joins the ranks of other sites that suffered over-whelming defeat in history, such as Massada and countless others. It has been the source of much modern-day retelling and analysis, and has even become the inspiration for a musical treatment by the Canadian group "La Nef," entitled *Montsegur*.

However, out of this tale of sadness comes a light of clarity that will provide an answer in this search for information about the Grail Hallows. Ean and Deike Begg, in their book *In Search of the Holy Grail and the Precious Blood*, suggest that the paintings in Montreal de SOS, as well as another name for the Cathars—"patarins" or "patarini" (meaning "People of the Cup"), demonstrate a definite link between the Cathars and the Grail Hallows. The Beggs provide the following account of how items sacred to the Cathars, possibly including the Grail itself, was removed from the besieged fortress to safety by members of the Cathar brotherhood.

> According to the witnesses at the Inquisition, on the night before the massacre, four Parfaits, Amiel Aicart, Hugues, Paytavi and another, whose name is unknown, who had hidden in a cave in the mountain beneath the stronghold, were lowered on ropes and made their escape. It seems most probable that whatever sacred objects were necessary for the celebration of the Feast of Bema—and they may have included service books, the Cathar Gospel of Saint John, a cup, a crystal for focusing the rays of the spring sun, or even the Tarot deck in which Cathar Gnosis is concealed—were removed for safe-keeping at the last moment [Begg, p. 54–55].

Those who made up the "heretical" sect known as the Cathars were a people who practiced what so many others preached, endeavoring to lead a clean life in dedication to God. Demonized by the Roman Catholic Church, either for what they believed in or for what they possessed, the Cathars became outcasts and were burned alive, as were their more military-minded associates, the Knights Templar. Because they knew they were not a part of the accepted body of the Christian church, the Cathars took their teachings into hiding, in the form of hidden meanings and secret indoctrination rituals which none but those who belonged to this outcast group could understand.

Before the Cathar heresy could be "cleansed" by the Pope's fires, a few of their numbers removed the heart of the Cathar doctrine from the path of the oncoming threat and preserved it as best they could—perhaps by hiding it in plain sight. Taking their rituals, customs, and stories with them, it is possible that the Cathars combined them all into one form that one may still find today, although not in any history book or public library. The Cathar's view of, and history with, the Grail Hallows may be written in the language of secrecy—as pictures that seem to have nothing to do with the story of Christ's Passion.

The Tarot deck is often considered a parlor game, used for amusement by some and an instrument of divination by others. To some, however, this simple game seems to speak of more important things, perhaps about forgotten knowledge. Furthermore, there exists a story about the Grail that, if one looks for it, uses the Tarot deck as its main characters. This story too seems to hint at something important yet unspoken. As with the Grail itself, one need only ask, and the mysteries can be revealed.

11

La Folie Perceval

Legends such as that of the Holy Grail and the Grail Hallows are quite possibly the worst kinds of subjects to approach from a historical standpoint. The difficulty in trying to find some historical "proof" for such a thing is enormous. It is not of the same caliber as trying to prove whether or not George Washington truly chopped down one of his father's cherry trees, nor would it be like trying to prove Atlantis existed. This legend lies somewhere in between.

However, this is not to say the pieces that comprise this vast and elaborate saga are not diverse. It might be thought of in terms of a great soup pot—boiling with the flavors, colors and textures of its many different ingredients, but nearly impossible to tell, just by looking, what those ingredients are. Through the erosion of time, the Grail and its associated relics have become the very image of *myth*. For that reason, finding definite historical fact is difficult, but it can be quite surprising at times as well.

This investigation has already crossed several different, distinct facets of history, making the claim that they all appear to be in some ways related. These assertions may be hard to accept when one first considers them. For example, it would seem unlikely that the "fortune-telling" Tarot, the heretical Cathars and Templars, Arthur's Merlin, and the Grail legend could all be smaller pieces of a larger historical tradition. It very nearly sounds like a bad conspiracy theory treatise at a New Age festival. It would certainly be unreasonable, and unscholarly, to make such an allegation—if it were not for one little-known text telling the traditional Grail story, but with a distinctively non-traditional flavor. This Grail story follows the progression of images now seen in the Tarot card deck almost exactly.

Before introducing this peculiar text, it is first necessary to become familiar with the Tarot deck itself and its history. Although some who study the Tarot claim it to be quite old (even pre-dating the time of Christ), the most accepted period ascribed to the birth of the traditional Tarot is the fourteenth century. Despite this "accepted" date, some still see the origins of the Tarot as being more than just an artistic gift for a king.

> We shall see in due course that the history of Tarot cards is largely of a negative kind, and that, when the issues are cleared by the dissipation of reveries and gratuitous speculations expressed in the terms of certitude, there is in fact no history prior to the fourteenth century. The deception and self-deception regarding their origin in Egypt, India or China put a lying spirit into the mouths of the first expositors, and the later occult writers have done little more than reproduce the first false testimony in the good faith of an intelligence unawakened to the issues of research. As it so happens, all expositions have worked within a very narrow range, and owe, comparatively speaking, little to the inventive faculty. One brilliant opportunity has at least been missed, for it has not so far occurred to any one that the Tarot might perhaps have done duty and even originated as a secret symbolical language of the Albigensian sects [The Pictorial Key to the Tarot, Arthur Edward Waite, pp. 7–8].

The first apparent Tarot deck was created in 1393 by the painter Charles Gringonneur, allegedly to placate the mentally ill King Charles VI of France. Now only a portion of this deck remains intact. In the Bibliotheque du Roi in Paris, one can still see the Fool, Emperor, Pope, Lovers, Wheel of Fortune, Temperance, Fortitude, Justice, Moon, Sun, Chariot, Hermit, Hanged Man, Death, Tower and Last Judgment cards, which are painted on a background of gold and silver, devoid of description or number, and more closely resembling the illuminations one might find in a medieval Book of Days than the mysterious Tarot. Examples of the Gringonneur deck's Minor Arcana "court cards" can also be found in the Musee Carrer in Venice.

Although this is the first "accepted" Tarot deck, its appearance is strikingly different than that of almost any other Tarot deck—certainly quite different than the Marseilles Deck, which has become the "standard" image of older Tarot cards. The fact that they are un-numbered and lack any name, explanation or other descriptor, suggests that these images once existed in some other form outside of the infamous Tarot cards. The flavor of the images presented in these, more artistic cards also suggests that they are intended to please the eye more than convey a secret message or a hidden meaning. Their similarity to other forms of medieval art would indicate that they may have been created from (or, more correctly, been inspired by) other simple images that either lacked a clear explanation or possessed a meaning that was not immediately readable.

Today the modern derivative of the Tarot deck looks quite different from that which originally offered the mysterious and cryptic images of the Devil and the Hanged Man. Though these images can still be found in current Tarot cards, the true modern offspring of the Tarot is not a Tarot deck at all, but a simple deck of playing cards. While some dispute this theory, the evidence seems quite clear. The modern deck of playing cards consists of four suits—clubs, spades, diamonds, and hearts. Similarly, each suit contains three "court" cards, dropping the Knight, and keeping the King, Queen, and Page (or "Jack"). Each pack of cards today also includes one other carry-over from the old Tarot deck—the Joker or Jester, also known as the Fool. Just as with the Fool card in the Tarot deck, this card remains unnumbered. While modern decks invariably include *two* Joker cards, both are of the same, singular figure. Although the mysterious images present in the Major Arcana are almost completely gone, the most important images, those of the Grail Hallows themselves, remain intact.

> The resources of interpretation have been lavished, if not exhausted, on the twenty-two Trumps Major, the symbolism of which is unquestionable. There remain the four suits, being Wands or Sceptres— *ex hypothesi*, in the archaeology of the subject, the antecedents of Diamonds in modern cards: Cups, corresponding to Hearts; Swords, which answer to Clubs, as the weapon of chivalry is in relation to the peasant's quarter-staff or the Alsatian bludgeon; and, finally, Pentacles—called also Deniers and Money—which are prototypes of Spades. In the old as in the new suits, there are ten numbered cards, but in the Tarot there are four Court Cards allocated to each suit, or a Knight in addition to King, Queen and Knave. The Knave is a page, valet, or *damoiseau*; most correctly, he is an esquire, presumably in the service of the Knight; but there are certain rare sets in which the page becomes a maid of honour, thus pairing the sexes in the tetrad of the court cards [Waite, pp. 31–32].

It is easy to see the close ties between the modern deck of playing cards and the enigmatic images of the Tarot. To some, there is still a stigma attached to the modern deck of playing cards to this day. Some denominations of Christian churches refuse to sanction the mere possession of playing cards. During the Civil War, soldiers who engaged in gambling in their camps would burn their playing cards before going into battle, lest they incur the wrath of God. Feelings regarding the Tarot deck run deep— deep enough to suggest that emotions have raged over these images for quite some time, perhaps even centuries. To illustrate the idea that the Tarot images are somewhat older than the traditional date, one need only look to another creation of the fourteenth century, predating the Gringonneur deck by 63 years, in which these images can be found, although in narrative instead of artistic imagery.

Written in A.D. 1330, *La Folie Perceval* retells the story of Perceval and his finding of the Holy Grail, and his witnessing the Grail procession in which the other Hallows can be seen. What makes this text remarkable is not simply the story it tells, but the manner in which the manuscript tells it. As the story progresses, Perceval (described as "Perceval the Fool" by the text's title) encounters several different strange characters who, upon a close reading, present a striking resemblance to the characters portrayed in the images of the Tarot deck's Major Arcana. This curiosity is not merely "reading into" the story. If one uses the Major Arcana of the Tarot deck as a "checklist," the order in which these characters are introduced seems to follow the sequence precisely. The following is paraphrased from Graham Phillips' book, *The Search for the Holy Grail.*

0. The Fool	Perceval is a young and naïve man who must learn to be wise to become the Grail guardian.
1. The Magician	Perceval encounters the Red Knight (later revealed to be Merlin), who challenges him to a duel. Perceval loses, but is offered a year in which to learn how to defeat the knight (the *Sir Gawain and the Green Knight* theme).
2. The Popess	Perceval meets a wise old woman who tells him how to find the castle of the Fisher King. He again encounters this woman after he fails to ask the Fisher King the right question. It is then when she makes her statement, "I was once as he who sent you here. I am the eagle who flew higher than any who dwelt in Rome. It is I who drank the wine of Peter and Joseph both."
3. The King 4. Queen	Perceval finally meets the Fisher King and his Queen (who is almost never seen in traditional Grail Romances). During a feast held in their presence, the Grail Hallows are seen in the Grail procession—the meaning of each object is

	later explained to Perceval by the wise old woman of the forest.
5. The Pope	Sometimes called the "Heirophant," the Pope can be seen in terms of Perceval's failure to ask the question. Some books about the Tarot state that this card indicates bad or incorrect advice. Therefore, this card's significance can be witnessed in the Old Knight's advice to Perceval that he should not ask too many questions.
6. The Lovers	Perceval then begins his path of learning how to become a knight by means of completing several quests. First, he encounters two lovers under a tree who ask him to obtain a golden apple from a giant.
7. The Chariot	Next, he meets a charioteer who holds a bleeding lance.
8. Justice	Although not stated, it can be assumed that Perceval wins his travails by the Right of Arms—the notion that a knight who defeats another knight in combat over a dispute is the knight who fought for the side of right and justice.
9. The Hermit	Perceval then meets a hermit, who reveals to him a vision of the Crucifixion.
10. Wheel of Fortune 11. Fortitude 12. Hanged Man	The vision of Christ suffering on the cross is reflected in these three images. The Wheel of Fortune indicates the changing of good times to bad; Fortitude is represented by Christ's statements during His trial; and the Hanged Man would seem to represent Christ while hanging on the cross. The crossed legs shown on this card has been thought to signify either the cross itself or a depiction of another form of crucifixion in which the victim is crucified upside down, sometimes with bent knees.
13. Death	Perceval then sees a cloaked figure who kills the grass as he walks.

14. Temperance	Learning perseverance and self-sacrifice, Perceval finally finds the castle of the Fisher King once more.
15. The Devil 16. The Tower	When Perceval returns to the castle, he discovers that it has been reduced to ruin by a lightning bolt and cast down by the devil. Curiously, the Tower card is sometimes called "the House of God," and it is indeed portrayed as being destroyed by a bolt of lightening or a fireball.
17. The Star	Although Perceval could be considered to be the "star" of the Grail saga, the Star card is represented both in the luminous, shining book that the Fisher King presents to Perceval when he finally asks the question, and by the meaning of the card. The Star is often said to represent "hope" or "optimism"—a feeling the Fisher King, seeking release from his torment, would have felt when Perceval finally arrived.
18. The Moon	The Red Knight then returns to challenge Perceval. The Moon card is said to represent hidden things and deception; therefore, when Merlin reveals himself to be the Red Knight after the battle, the meaning of this card is fulfilled. The moon could also represent the passage of time, particularly the year's time the knight gave Perceval to learn how to become a true knight.
19. The Sun	The Sun card represents the idea that things will go your way. During the battle, the Red Knight again defeats Perceval by mortally wounding him with his sword. However, as the new Fisher King, Perceval cannot die and therefore wins the battle.
20. Judgment	Because Perceval stood before the Red Knight in battle and fought valiantly, the debt of honor was satisfied, and Perceval was judged worthy to become the new guardian of the Grail.

21. The World   Meant to represent "The New World" or
Heaven, this card stands both for Perceval
rebuilding the Grail castle, called the "White
Castle of the White Town," and for the book
of the Grail being carried to heaven by a "white
maiden" [Phillips, pp. 95–98].

Witnessing this nearly "algorithmic" procession of the Grail story, there can be little doubt that the writer of this text did so with the cards of the Tarot's Major Arcana in mind. Of course, the Minor Arcana consists of the Grail procession itself, and is depicted in an illustration found in La Folie Perceval—the Grail cup, the bleeding lance, the dish from the Last Supper (separate from the Grail), and the sword (in a covered box) that beheaded John the Baptist. Again recall that the suits pictured in the Minor Arcana were once called Cups, Bowls, Lances and Swords.

Now that this close association between the Grail text *La Folie Perceval* and the Tarot cards has been established, one must wonder about the text's antiquity. Although the manuscript itself can only be dated to the fourteenth century (around 1330), the story appears to be much older. The striking similarities between *La Folie Perceval* and a portion of an earlier work entitled *Fulke le Fitz Waryn*, written around 1260, lends credence to this assertion. Although this earlier text still dates from a time later than Chretien's "original" Grail story (which was still a work in progress until the time of his death in 1190), it does place it around the same time period given to the increase in Grail-related texts between the years 1190 and 1220.

While this dating of the Perceval narrative does not prove a connection between the Tarot and the sourcebook allegedly used by both Chretien and Wolfram, the mention of a character named "Payne Peveril" in the *Fulke le Fitz Waryn* takes the time period from which the story originates much further back, most likely to a year *pre-dating* Chretien's text. Phillips clearly outlines the links between the character of Payne Peveril in *Fulke le Fitz Waryn* and another, much earlier Welsh poem written around 1100, called simply *Peveril*.

> *La Folie Perceval* now survives in a manuscript preserved in the Biliotheque Nationale, Paris. Catalogued as MS *Fonds francais 12577*, the manuscript itself dates from around 1330 and contains a number of Arthurian tales copied by the same anonymous scribe. As other stories in the manuscript are prose versions of earlier Arthurian poems, such as Wace's *Roman de Brut* and Chretien's *Lancelot*, it seems that the scribe was attempting to translate into prose all the early Arthurian

romances. The sources for the other works still survive in earlier copies, although an original *Folie* has not yet been discovered. The reason for believing that it may have been based on the same romance as the *Peveril* sections in *Fulke le Fitz Waryn*, however, is that the opening lines of both are almost identical.

The *Peveril* section of *Fulke le Fitz Waryn* opens with Merlin's prediction concerning the coming of a great warrior:

> The leopard will follow the wolf,
> And with his tail will threaten him.
> The wolf will leave the woods and mounts,
> Will remain in the water with the fishes,
> And will pass over the sea,
> Will encircle the whole island,
> At last he will conquer the leopard
> By his cunning and by his art;
> Then he will come into this land
> Will have his stronghold in the water.

The *Folie* begins with virtually the same prophecy:

> The leopard will follow the wolf, and will threaten him with his tail and drive him into the sea. But the wolf will return from the sea to conquer the leopard by stealth and by cunning. Then he will come to the White Land and build his castle on an island in a lake.

In *Fulk le Fitz Waryn* the passage is seen as a prophecy concerning Fulk's quarrel with King John, and his ultimate possession of Wittingon Castle. In the *Folie* the same prophesy is said to refer to Perceval's quarrel with a Red Knight, and his eventual building of a new Grail castle in the White Town [Phillips, pp. 94–95].

Similarities between Perceval, the original Grail hero, and *Fulke le Fitz Waryn*'s Payne Peveril, Fulke's great-grandfather, suggest that they might be one and the same. But it's not just the name of the hero that suggests this association. The *Didcot Perceval*, written around 1200, states that Perceval's father is called "Alain li Gros," or "Alan of the Cross." Similarly, the story of Payne Peveril in *Fulke le Fitz Waryn* names Peveril's father as "Alan le Crux"—again "Alan of the Cross."

Phillips goes on to demonstrate that not only were Peveril Payne and his father historical people, but they were also connected to another name of some importance to this investigation—Blayse.

> Payne Peveril and his father were not fictional characters, they were real historical figures. Both their names and Payne Peveril's lordship of Whittington are recorded in the Domesday Book and in the twelfth-century *Feet of Fines*. Equally, not only was Peveril a contemporary of the St. Asaph Blayse, but the records of St. Asaph Abbey show that Blayse actually became the priest of Whittington in 1090. It is surely

> beyond coincidence that the most likely author of the original Grail
> story, adapted by the author of the *Didcot Perceval*, was Payne Peveril's
> personal chaplain [p. 90].

In *The Search for the Grail*, Phillips asserts that the Blaise of legend,
the original writer of the Grail saga, is actually an eleventh-century monk
named Blayse from the abbey of St. Asaph in northern Wales. Considering the description of Blaise from the thirteenth century *Prose Merlin* and
The Suite du Merlin, this raises a conundrum. If the eleventh-century Blayse
from the abbey of St. Asaph is the same person as the Blaise who allegedly
was Merlin's contemporary in the sixth century, there can be one of two
explanations—either this monk himself drank from the life-prolonging
Grail, or the association with Merlin in the sixth century was the result of
the writer, either as a literary tool or a simple error.

Phillips claims this error of placement in time was just that—an error.
He maintains that the contemporaneous placement of both Blaise (or
Blayse) and Perceval was the result of two separate traditions regarding
whose family had the responsibility of guarding the Grail, Perceval's or
Arthur's. Although it does, in fact, appear that the fourteenth century *La
Folie Perceval* was inspired by, and drew from, a much earlier poem called
Peveril, this sort of error seems unlikely.

> It seems likely that the *Folie* is a fairly accurate rendering of the
> original poem, since none of the other stories contained in the
> manuscript have been elaborated by the copyist, merely translated into
> prose. Accordingly, it may be a close rendition of the first medieval
> Grail romance [Phillips, p. 95].

The final line of this quote offers an answer to this paradox: The poem *Peveril* may mark the point at which history books regarding the Grail were
used to create the medieval Grail romance.

The only medieval reference to Alain and Perceval (or Peveril) comes
from a time closer to the medieval Grail romancers than to Arthur and his
quest. Indeed, Phillips correctly states that there is no clear evidence to
support a character from that time period that could account for the creation of the Perceval character. What is clear, however, is that there was a
Grail tradition at Whittington, and that the mysterious riddle that lead
Phillips to the grotto at Hawkstone Park was created to hide something of
immense value at the time. Although it does seem likely that the character of Perceval is native to the eleventh century, it would appear just as likely
that Blaise was contemporary to Arthur and Merlin rather than the eleventh
century. *The Prose Merlin* goes so far as to say that Blaise was the priest who
served as confessor to Merlin's mother. It is unlikely that this depth of

detail is the result of mere confusion. Although the *Folie* does not include *The Prose Merlin* or *The Suite du Merlin*, it does contain Wace's *Roman de Brut*, which appears to have inspired the two later works.

Thus it is reasonable to infer that Blayse of St. Asaph was not the Blaise to whom Merlin dictated the original saga of the Grail and the Hallows, and that the character of Perceval, the original Grail hero of medieval romance, was a contemporary to this eleventh century Welsh monk. It is possible that Blayse did write the poem *Peveril* using the earlier Grail histories (consisting of the Blaise text and perhaps some others), and, in so doing, created the first Grail *romance*.

It would appear that the author of *La Folie Perceval* not only used the poem *Peveril* to create his Grail story, but also the images now found in the Tarot deck. The subject of the Grail saga, the Grail Hallows, appear as the suits of the cards found in the Minor Arcana, and the mysterious characters that the apparently eleventh century Perceval encounters are represented by the images found in the Major Arcana. Therefore, one must wonder what inspired this writer to create a Tarot image–based Grail story, which itself included a poem written in A.D. 1100, pre-dating the traditionally held origin of the Grail legend of 1190.

If the genesis of this enigmatic text is to be fully understood, one must find a historical location where the Grail tradition, the Tarot, early Grail histories dating from the time of Merlin and Blaise, and the images of the Grail Hallows co-existed together. Only in the region of southern France, made famous by the Cathar traditions at Montsegur and the cave painting at Montreal de SOS, can such a place be found. If the Cathars chose to use the Hallows in their imagery and teaching, their role in the Grail legend may have found its way to the author of the *Folie* in the form of an enigmatic sourcebook that may have been the inspiration for the entire body of medieval Grail romances. What might this sourcebook have looked like? What could it have contained?

12

The "Folio" Perceval

Following its own tempestuous nature, the early Middle Ages was a time of odd combinations of symbols and traditions, as well as hidden meanings and mysteries. Having just emerged from the Dark Ages, Europe was filled with legends, myths, and competing theologies—all subject to the judgment of the Roman Catholic Church. Although some historians might argue that the Church created its own set of mysterious rites and traditions (some of which seem downright bizarre, given today's perspective), all would agree that the Roman Catholic Church viewed itself as the standard by which all other traditions must abide. Variation from this meant harsh punishment and even death.

Just as the early Christian church was forced to hide its teachings in symbols such as the fish, heretical sects were forced to hide their doctrine in other forms as well. The Templars, made famous during the Crusades, began to speak in terms of mathematics and building, creating mysterious and beautiful masterpieces of architecture (such as the Roslyn Chapel in Scotland) filled with an odd mixture of pagan, Christian, and Templar motifs. Other groups turned to works of art, using paintings and sculpture to hide their hidden doctrines. And no group better encapsulates the mystery and silence of these early heretical sects than the Cathars.

The Cathars are known to have created many enigmatic works, ranging from paintings to cryptic cave art to beautiful books—their secrets locked within the minds of their long-dead creators. Although modern historians and archeologists can make educated guesses, it is impossible to know completely the meaning and intention of these works without some sort of codex. Although every student of history thinks wistfully of the Rosetta Stone in these cases, the sad truth is that such code keys are seldom, if ever, found.

Even though this fact casts a shadow over historical research, one may come as near as is possible by considering these encoded works of art in context. A knowledge of what came after allows one to gain some understanding of what these paintings and writings might have meant, and what they tell about other things happening at that time. It would seem that the Cathars hid their secret doctrine in a variety of forms that likely included the images now used in the deck of cards known as the Tarot. It is also clear that, like their close compatriots the Templars, the Cathars were thought to have possessed great Christian relics.

It is here that the investigation into the histories of the Cathars and the Tarot deck come into focus regarding the legend of the Grail Hallows. A cursory glimpse of the Tarot indicates a link between the Grail Hallows and the suits of the Tarot deck, as well as some of the cards from the Major Arcana. It is also clear that whomever wrote *La Folie Perceval* did so with the Major Arcana of the Tarot in mind, with the story following the procession of images from the Tarot one by one. It has been thought that the *Folie* manuscript was at least based on, if not taken from, an earlier manuscript that is quite likely older than the text written by Chretien de Troyes in 1190.

In her book *From Ritual to Romance*, published in 1920, Jessie Weston postulated that a link existed between the four suits of the Tarot deck and the four Grail Hallows. Since then, another theory has evolved regarding the Tarot in relation to the Hallows. Some think that not only was the Tarot deck a part of the Grail and Hallows story, it was also a pictorial book created as a teaching guide for the Cathar doctrine. Some early Grail texts describe the Grail as not only a vessel of some kind, but also a book—a book that not just anyone can read. It is quite possible that this book, as well as the mysterious "sourcebook" upon which Chretien and Wolfram von Eschenbach based their very different accounts of the Grail story, may have been just such an encrypted tool, decipherable only by those who knew how to interpret its symbols and recreate its meaning.

If the book that only the indoctrinated could read was in fact this pictorial book, created by the Cathars using the images that have now become the cards of the Tarot, this would mean that the Cathars in some way, for some reason, based their doctrine on the legendary Grail and its Hallows. To understand how the Cathars are tied to the Hallows, a few things must be considered. Firstly, they were seen as being close to the Knights Templar—even to the point that the Templars defended them against allegations of heresy. Second, the Cathars were thought to be in possession of very important Christian relics. In fact, when the last Cathar bastion at Montsegur fell, tradition states that several of their order fled the mountain fortress with either the Grail or a relic closely associated with it. Lastly, the Cathars are thought to have been influenced by an earlier heretical movement that was also associated with the Grail legend—Pelagianism.

Although there is no way of knowing definitely how closely they followed the beliefs and writings of the earlier Pelagians, it is clear that the Cathars used symbols similar to the Grail Hallows in their initiation rites and rituals, as well as sharing the Pelagians' views on the value of chastity, poverty, etc. One may see how the Cathars, considering the Pelagians the rightful heirs to the Christian tradition by way of certain relics of Christ's Passion, would have adopted the belief systems of the Pelagians and incorporated them into their existing culture. If the Cathars did indeed possess the Grail or something related to it, the Pelagians' story and writings may very well have been carried along with the object of veneration, just as the previously mentioned Grail text stated.

If one still doubts the connection between the Cathars and the Grail Hallows, especially in the form of the suits of the Tarot deck, history and archeology have fortunately provided another piece of evidence to substantiate this theory. Near the cities of Montsegur and Lombrives there is a cave under the ruins of the castle Montreal de SOS. Any hearty adventurer willing to go there will discover a rather unusual sight.

> Beneath the last remaining wall of the castle is a cave with two entrances or exits. On the wall of the cave a remarkable painting was discovered in 1932 by Joseph Mandement, president of the Syndicat d'Initiative of Tarascon, and two friends. It shows a lance, a broken sword, a solar disk, many red crosses (as worn by the Templars) and a square panel (40cm by 40cm), rather like a table-cloth. It has an outer part with twenty crosses—eighteen white and two red, eleven Saint Andrew's and nine Greek—on a black background. An inner square contains five tear-shaped red drops of blood and five white crosses. If we take the central square as the *taillover* (dish) described by Chretien de Troyes, we have here all the elements carried in the Grail procession. Here was the missing link between the Cathars in the last strongholds of Langeudoc and the Holy Grail [Begg, *In Search of the Holy Grail and the Precious Blood*, p. 57].

One can see that the Cathars likely used images of the cup, the dish or bowl, the sword, and the lance in their artwork, and obviously in their initiation rites. Therefore, it is easy to accept the idea that the suits of the Tarot are in some way based on the Grail Hallows, and were used by the Cathars to perpetuate their doctrine and teachings.

One may then wonder, if the Cathars used this pictorial teaching book based on the Grail Hallows, the images later becoming the Tarot deck,

The enigmatic painting found in a cave under the ruins of Montreal de S.O.S. Apparently linked to Cathar activity and teaching in the area, this painting depicts many of the relics that comprise the Grail Hallows—the lance at the top of the picture, the sword in the middle right, and a disk that could represent the bowl just to the left of the sword. The

from where did their Hallow-based doctrine originate? Also, when did they begin using this teaching method, and why? To answer these questions, one must look back to the earlier heresy from which they took their ideals. If the Cathars were influenced by Pelagianism, they would have learned of the Grail Hallows from there, since the relics of Christ's Passion were central to the Pelagians' claim as the true Christian church.

One problem remains with this assumption. The only relics that the Pelagian church (that is, the church in Britain in the fifth century) were known to possess were the two vials of blood and sweat carried by Joseph of Arimathea from Israel to Britain after Christ's crucifixion,

bottom half of the painting appears to have some meaning, and since it seems to contain six drops of blood, it could be assumed that this is meant to represent the most holy of the Grail Hallows, the Grail chalice itself. *Above:* Philippe Contal's representation of the cave painting, showing details more clearly: Note that the entire image is surrounded by crosses, as well as the inner border of the square that might represent the Grail as a container for blood relics. Although the sword appears to be represented intact, with the blade unbroken, research conducted by Ean and Deike Begg seems to suggest that the sword was at some point shown broken. (Photograph and illustration courtesy of Philippe Contal, www.cathares.org.)

and the "Marian Chalice" sent to Britain in A.D. 410 from Rome. There is no evidence suggesting that the lance or the sword was ever in Britain (nor even any mention of same). Does this paradox invalidate the theory that the Cathars took their teachings from the Pelagians? Absolutely not. Not only does this fail to disprove the theory, it helps place the Cathar's Tarot book in time, showing exactly when they began using the images of the Hallows in their teachings.

To place these images in the Cathar teachings, one must look back to the source, and the first two relics found at Britain. Joseph is thought to have brought the two vials to Britain around A.D. 40 to 70, with the Marian Chalice arriving about 410. Around this time, Pelagius was excommunicated by the Roman Catholic Church while he was in Africa. To his followers, Rome sending the Marian Chalice to the church in Britain would have constituted an unofficial acknowledgement of their claim to be a valid church at least, and God's divine justice in the attacks on Rome at most. This would surely earn a place in the history of the British church.

Advancing in time now to the sixth century in Britain (the time of King Arthur), the first written story of the Grail Hallows is allegedly penned. According to the *Prose Merlin*, written by Robert de Baron around 1200, this first account of the Grail and Hallows was recounted by Merlin and written by an individual named Blaise (or sometimes Blayse or Blois), who was Merlin's mother's confessor and priest. The following passage from the *Prose Merlin* describes the account of Merlin narrating the story of the Grail, and Blaise writing it down.

> But now believe what I shall tell you about faith in Jesus Christ. I shall tell what no one else, save God alone, could tell you. Make it into a book; and many people, hearing it read, will be better for it and save themselves from sin, and you will thus be performing an act of great charity. ...
>
> When Blais was prepared, Merlin gave him a faithful account of the love that Jesus Christ and Joseph [of Arimathea] had shown each other, and told him the story of Alain and his companions, and how Joseph had relinquished the Grail and then died...

A few paragraphs later in the text, another passage makes the manuscript Blaise writes sound even more like our mysterious sourcebook.

> Just as I live hidden, and always shall, from those to whom I do not wish to reveal myself, so, too, the book will remain obscure and only rarely will anyone reap all its benefit.

This passage seems to indicate that this book, either in form or in content, will be in some way obscured—hidden from the many for the benefit of the few select. Finally, the writer of the *Prose Merlin* has some knowledge of what became of this book (in a way putting words in Merlin's mouth).

> And so the book of Joseph, the book of the lineages that I have told you about, will be put together with your book and mine; your labor will have been completed and you will be worthy of their company. Your book, then, will be joined to that of Joseph, as clear evidence of the work that you and I have done. If they like it, they will show their thankfulness and pray for us to our Lord. The two books together will make a single fine book and will be of equal worth—except in this respect: that I cannot and must not relate the private words that passed between Joseph and Jesus Christ [Wilhelm, *The Romance of Arthur*, pp. 316–317].

From this one would infer that the sourcebook, which in some Grail texts is actually called the Grail, came in some way from this text written by Blaise, detailing the origin of the Grail and the other Hallows. However, the only sourcebook discussed thus far is one much like the medieval *Biblia Pauperum*, a pictorial Bible—only the sourcebook would have been created using the images now seen in the Tarot deck. But several aspects of the Tarot images, and the Cathar links to them, indicate that this Tarot-based sourcebook came from a later time.

The answer to this riddle is clear. Since the Cathars were influenced by the much earlier Pelagians, reason dictates that their texts and traditions would have been part of that influence. Therefore, the text written by Blaise (which one may assume was written in the last half of the fifth century, since Merlin is said to have been born around 450) would have become part of the Cathar's venerated books—just as the passage from the *Prose Merlin* indicated (by stating that this book would later be joined with other books).

To fully understand how the story of the Grail Hallows was passed down through history, it is necessary to draw a parallel between the Pelagians of the fifth century and the Blaise manuscript, and the Cathars of southern France who came 500 years after them. Using historical and archeological facts, it is possible to determine how and when the original story of the Hallows, as told by Merlin, became the Cathar's Tarot-based sourcebook used to create *La Folie Perceval*. The following outlines the evolution of the Cathar sourcebook from its origins in England through its now familiar form of the Tarot card deck.

The manuscript passed to the Cathars would have been a later copy of the text written by Blaise, having been illustrated and possibly mixed with earlier histories of Joseph and the first church at Glastonbury. Curiously, it is the illustrations in this book, originally intended as mere accom-

LE · MAT

The Fool

paniment for the text, that will propagate the story. The sequence of the images would not have come in strict historical order, but in the order as dictated by the style of the writer. It was customary to begin a work by crediting those who came before, whether it be a mention of those who told the story before the writer, or as respect for one seen as the "creator" of the story, quite often referencing God as an initial "prayer."

If the researcher makes the unconfirmable but certainly reasonable assumptions that Joseph did in fact carry his two vials to Britain to start the church at Glastonbury, and that Merlin and Blaise were familiar with, if not members of, the Pelagian movement, one can see how the Blaise manuscript was written with a knowledge of the events of Pelagius' visit to Rome and subsequent excommunication. Either in an attempt to honor him, or as the result of later combining with other books (as stated in the *Prose Merlin*), the story written by Blaise can be considered the first version of the sourcebook, covering the events between Joseph's arrival at Britain through Pelagius' confrontation with the Church (resulting in his excommunication), and Rome sending the Marian Chalice to Britain.

The first image would have been that of Joseph of Arimathea. Likely he would have been portrayed as either leaving on a long journey or standing on a hill (namely, Wearyal Hill near Glastonbury), carrying his two vials. Although the image of "the Fool" in the Tarot deck is usually portrayed as a young man, he is seen carrying his possessions with him, and in other Tarot decks is portrayed as standing atop a cliff or mountain. The dog also visible in the image is thought to portray the idea of "dogs nipping at your heels." It is interesting to remember that Joseph and his company left Israel after being imprisoned and threatened by the Romans and Sanhedrin elders. Curiously, this card is the only one among the Major Arcana without a number, indicating that it is the beginning card, or card of initiation. One may assume that since this was in itself a long story, this image may have been embedded amid a great and expansive text.

The Magician

The tale then formally begins with Merlin outlining the story of the Grail and Hallows. The first card of the Major Arcana, "the Magician," is seen standing before a table covered with the tools of his trade. However, the table also contains the symbols for the four suits of the Minor Arcana—the pentacles or bowls, the lance or staff, the cup, and the sword in the

LA · PAPESSE

The Popess or Priestess

form of a small knife. In the context of the Blaise manuscript, this would have been the illustration which made Merlin, who was seen as magical (a Magician), the formal chronicler of the story, telling how the Grail came to Britain, and how the Marian Chalice (the bowl) was sent to Britain from Rome, as well as how the lance played a part in the Crucifixion. Since the Pelagians valued the Old Testament as much as the New Testament, the story of John the Baptist (the last prophet of the Mosaic Laws), who was beheaded with a sword, was represented by inclusion of the sword in the Grail Hallows.

The tale then continues with the second part of the story—that of the Marian Chalice being found and sent to Britain, as well as how Pelagius went before the Roman Catholic Church. This story of how the *second* Grail comes to Britain begins with Constantine the Great's mother, Helena, visiting Jerusalem in search of important sites in the life and death of Christ. Learning the location of Christ's tomb, she discovers that the tomb has been obscured by a temple dedicated to the goddess Aphrodite, at the center of which stands a marble statue of the goddess herself. Therefore, in the context of the Blaise manuscript, the Tarot card of "the Priestess" or "Popess" (which could be extended to the term "goddess") would have been used to denote the temple of Aphrodite being torn down to reach the tomb of Christ.

The focal point of the next part of the story is Helena herself. Although she was mother to the Emperor Constantine, she took the title "Helena Augusta," making herself the Empress of Rome. It is not surprising, therefore, that in the Tarot deck "the Empress" comes before "the Emperor." Helena did in fact play a role in the story of the Hallows and the Grail *before* her son the Emperor. In the tomb of Christ she discovered many artifacts of the Crucifixion, including a portion of three crosses, one of which was that on which Jesus hung, as well as the nails with which He was crucified.

She then took these relics to Rome where they remained on display for many years. However, she sent the nails to her son. With them he created a bridle for his horse, included one in his helmet, and embedded one in a spear he had made—with which he allegedly drew out the boundaries of his new capital, Constantinople. It would seem that the church in Britain valued the empire created by Constantine in honor of, and based around the worship of, Jesus Christ.

The story then turns to Pelagius and his conflict with the Church. It

The Empress

IIII

L'EMPEREUR

The Emperor

would appear by his possible acceptance of the Constantinian church and his disdain for the Roman church that Pelagius confronted the Pope in part due to what he saw as an ever-increasing level of corruption. With this in mind, the Major Arcana card called "the Pope" appears quite striking. The image shows the much larger Pope looming ominously over the two smaller figures that represent Pelagius himself and his companion Caelestius, pleading their case before the Pope.

Under threat of excommunication, Pelagius ultimately had to choose between his church in Britain and its doctrine, and the Roman Church and the ruling of the Pope. This forced choice is reflected in the next card of the Major Arcana, "the Lovers." Here we see a man forced to choose between an old love and a new one, with the price for a wrong decision coming swiftly from above, most likely from God.

It is interesting here to recall the archetypal stories in medieval literature of the knight and the old hag, which usually involved the knight being forced to choose between a lover who is old but faithful, and one who is young but devious. The knight, giving the choice over to another, makes the right decision and wins a lover who is both young and beautiful, yet faithful to the end. It also brings to mind the medieval notion of the old hag on a dragon, representing Judaism, and a young maiden on a lion, representing Christianity. (Perhaps it was in part the Roman Church's hatred for the claims made by the British church that caused this seemingly misplaced animosity toward the Jewish religion.)

Finally choosing what he feels is right, Pelagius returns to his church in Britain, despite the curse placed on him by Rome. However, history speaks of a certain amount of retribution paid to Rome for its decision. In A.D. 410, Rome was attacked by barbarian invaders, and, as a result, the Marian Chalice found by Helena in Christ's tomb was sent to Britain for safety—most likely to Glastonbury (since it was known to already house sacred relics of the Passion). This divine justice is represented in the Major Arcana by the card known as "the Chariot." Both the chario-

The Pope

teer and the horses appear to be in some way supernatural, so one would infer that this represents God's wrath come to Rome. Interestingly, the front of the chariot is blazoned with the letters "SM." It is possible that this stands for "Sacra Maria," referring to the Marian Chalice sent to Britain from Rome.

The Lovers

This marks the end of the Blaise manuscript and its story of the Grail Hallows. One can clearly see that not all images from the modern Tarot deck are present. Absent is the rest of the Major Arcana, as well as the entire Minor Arcana (in which the actual artifacts are shown). However, one must realize that this original book and its illustrations were a simple history, not yet meant to be any sort of teaching tool. That role would only come later, in the twelfth century, when this original illustrated history would evolve into something quite different. Though probably cryptic in nature, it was not a purposefully enigmatic folio (as it would later become when the Cathars made it into its final form).

It is also likely that this source is how the legend of the Grail and the Hallows entered fully into the Celtic mythology. Although magical cauldrons and other similarities surely existed in Celtic folk stories prior to this, the Blaise manuscript is quite possibly where the story *Peredur* originated. Since the *Mabinogion* dates positively from the fifteenth century, this sixth-century version written by Blaise (or some close derivation thereof) might have been included with the older stories from the oral tradition. This would also explain why the story from Chretien's sourcebook matched so closely the beginning of

Peredur. Since the beginning of both stories are almost identical but vary later in the text, this would suggest the author of *Peredur* drew from the same text as would Chretien in later centuries, but was forced to extrapolate for the remainder of the text.

The story of the Hallows remained in this form, the property of the British church, for centuries. It is unclear how the manuscript made its way into the hands of the early Cathar sect, but one may assume that since the early roots of Catharism took hold in the soil prepared by Pelagianism, some of the early, defining documentation was shared. Since early Catharism was seen as far north as Germany, and was present in both Spain and Italy, it is likely that it also reached as far as Glastonbury.

Perhaps due to pressure from the Roman Church, or perhaps based on their knowledge of past groups deemed heretical, the Cathars became a closed group—teaching their doctrine in private, and using secret codes and symbols (as seen in the cave beneath the mountain fortress of Montreal de SOS). One can picture the new Cathar initiate facing the wall painting, and being told its significance or reciting a type of Cathar catechism, demonstrating his knowledge of the hidden doctrine.

The Chariot

This painting proves to be of great importance to one investigating the history of the Grail Hallows. Not only is this painting associated with the Cathars, and depicts all the objects that comprise the Hallows, it is most important for its depiction of one item—the sword. Although it is not reflected in the painting now visible at Montreal de SOS, Deike and Ean Begg suggest in their book, *In Search of the Holy Grail and the Precious Blood*, that the sword in this cave painting was shown *broken*. This demonstrates something very important in dating the Cathar's introduction to the Grail Hallows.

It is around the beginning of the tenth century that the first definite traces of Catharism are recorded. It is also around this time that Otto the Great, the first Emperor of what was called the Holy Roman Empire, is said to have first possessed the relic now found in the Hoffberg Museum— allegedly the spearhead from the lance that pierced Christ's side. Called the Spear of Destiny to those familiar with the history of Adolph Hitler and the Third Reich, this relic has also been called the lance or the *sword* of St. Maurice.

The legend of St. Maurice holds that, as a Roman Legionnaire, Maurice was ordered to kill a group of Christians—men, women, and children— at the behest of the Roman Emperor. When he and his army refused, they were set upon by the Emperor's forces and all killed. His sword thus became an object of veneration to all those who claimed to be soldiers in the army of Christ. Since this relic in Austria has been called a sword in the past, it is possible that those who saw it for the first time in the tenth century heard of its sacredness and took it to be the sword that beheaded John the Baptist, especially if they were familiar with the Blaise manuscript (as the early Cathars seem to have been).

Some might think this would be an unlikely mistake to make, considering it was not called "the sword that beheaded John the Baptist," but rather, "the sword of St. Maurice." However, one must understand the peculiar set of circumstances at play in this situation. Consider for a moment that an early Cathar, having just read about John the Baptist in the Blaise manuscript, hears of a holy relic being housed in Germany. Perhaps compounding the confusion is the writing on the golden collar that joins the two halves of the spear together stating that it is the lance used to pierce Christ's side at the Crucifixion.

This Cathar (or some of his brothers) journeys to see this relic, full of reverence and piety, only to gaze upon something that looks quite like a Roman Gladius instead of a spearhead. Since the "True Lance of the Crucifixion" was also allegedly hidden away in Constantinople, these Cathars may well have jumped to the conclusion that this was the very sword used to behead the prophet John the Baptist. (The author must admit here that such a mistaken conclusion was reached by the author himself in a previous book regarding the history of the Holy Grail.)

To one familiar with the four Grail Hallows, it must have seemed like the circle was again complete—Joseph's vials were hidden at Glastonbury, the Marian Chalice accompanied them there, and the lance, although not in the possession of either the Cathars or the British church, was known to be in Constantinople. Now, with the introduction of this new relic, the "sword" in Germany, the four relics alluded to by the Blaise manuscript were in safe keeping.

Two things must be realized to understand why this is so important to the dating of the Cathar's inclusion of the Grail Hallows in their teachings. First, if the sword painted on the cave wall at Montreal de SOS was originally depicted as broken, as the Beggs' research states, this demonstrates that the sword was recognized as being the sword of John the Baptist after it was cut into two pieces. The first evidence of the Austrian relic being parted into two pieces comes from Otto I, the first Holy Roman Emperor, who made copies of the lance and had them sent to the kings of Hungary and Poland in the tenth century. Since these copies were also made as a lance head in two pieces, joined by a golden collar, the depiction of the broken sword in the cave painting can be placed no earlier than the tenth century. Second, since the Tarot deck's Minor Arcana shows the sword and the lance held by a hand emerging from a cloud or a ball of fire (presumably the hand of God), and the cup and the bowl are shown in a more earthly, physical setting, one may infer that the relics of the sword and lance were known to the British church and Cathars, but were not in their possession—rather in God's keeping.

The story of the Grail and the Hallows seemed to enjoy an unexplained popularity boost during the eleventh century. It is during this time that the early versions of *Peveril*, later included in *La Folie Perceval*, likely was written. It is the century from which most of the first literature and histories regarding Joseph of Arimathea, the Grail, and the Hallows was penned. It was also the century that saw Catharism rise to its full height. One may wonder what caused the significant increase in interest surrounding the Grail Hallows at this time. All of the early authors who wrote about the Hallows speak of a sourcebook from which they took their stories. Some even go so far as to label the book itself a part of the Grail.

To finally understand the legend of the Grail Hallows, one must again turn to its inconsistencies. Why are there sometimes two vessels present when referring to the Grail—both a cup and a bowl (or dish)? Why is the sword that beheaded John the Baptist present among relics specific to Jesus and His crucifixion? Finally, why are all these objects linked together, imbued with near-equal importance, in the Grail processions and other lists of sacred artifacts found in the Grail romances? To answer these questions, one must find the one point at which all these objects appeared together in the same place.

Proceeding by process of elimination, one can rule out Glastonbury and the early church known by either Joseph of Arimathea or Pelagius. They possessed only the original two vials belonging to Joseph, and the Marian Chalice sent to them from Rome. We can rule out the Roman Church, as they despised the notion of the Holy Grail and the other relics thought to be part of the Hallows. They possessed only the lance, and mostly kept it hidden away to stem the tide of every European nation during the Middle Ages claiming the right to power because they owned the "true lance." One can rule out, with some degree of certainty, the stories being a creation of pure fiction since the writings of the fifth century historian Olympiodorus mention the Marian Chalice. Furthermore, medieval writers would not have simply "thrown in" the sword that beheaded John the Baptist in a story about the relics of Christ's Passion.

All these facts together suggest an intriguing solution. The source-book from which the later works about the Grail and the Hallows arose was written by someone familiar enough with the relics at Glastonbury to mention that there were two vessels, a bowl from the Last Supper and a vessel that held Christ's blood, yet not familiar enough to know that the vessel containing the blood relic was not a chalice, but two unguentaria vials. The writer also mentions the lance, which was never at Glastonbury, and apparently places it in the hands of someone else, perhaps someone under God's protection, rather than in their own keeping. The writer also mentions a broken sword—a sword not involved with the death of Jesus as were the other relics, but with the death of John the Baptist, whose importance would have been less than that of Jesus to a medieval Christian, but considered of equal importance to a Pelagian who valued the Old Testament heroes as much as Jesus. The writer indicated the sword was broken because that was the form with which he was familiar, having seen what outwardly appeared to be a Roman Gladius sword, separated in two parts, in the court of Otto the Great or his heirs, thus placing them in the tenth or eleventh century. He knew this was not, in fact, the lance from the Crucifixion because Constantinople was known to possess the true lance, it having arrived there from Jerusalem where it had remained safely for several centuries.

This would make the writer of the sourcebook one who was familiar with the Pelagian tradition and history, removed from Britain, and contemporary with the spear in Germany—in short, an early Cathar. The sourcebook written by this Cathar would have been created in a somewhat cryptic form, one available only to other Cathars. A book made from the images now known as the Tarot would have fit this bill nicely. Therefore, it seems most likely from the evidence presented above that the sourcebook described by early Grail writers was, in fact, a Cathar book, one which started out as the simple narrative written by Blaise and later transformed into a book of indoctrination centered on the images now used in the Tarot deck.

This book was likely created as a kind of celebration or memorialization of the sword being found again in Germany, as well as to commemorate the early Grail and Hallows tradition. It was for this purpose, and for teaching new Cathar initiates seeking to learn God's truth, that the book was created in its final form. For this book, more images were created to form what is now known as the Major Arcana, around which revolved their moral teachings regarding their mortal lives, as well as their spiritual lives, ending with the final judgment before God as outlined in the book of Revelation. Entire groups of cards were based upon the four Hallows as markers of the initiate's journey along the path of learning. For each Hallow, a new set of lessons had to be learned.

The final, purely pictorial form of what this book might have looked like is presented in the following pages. The only way to evenly match all Minor Arcana cards with the Major Arcana cards is to place one suit of Minor around the first, un-numbered card of the Major. Then, making three rows of seven with the remaining numbered Major cards (as detailed in Italo Calvino's *The Castle of Crossed Destinies*), one places two Minor Arcana cards on either side of each Major. In this way, the following sequence was created.

Around the first card of the Major Arcana, "the Fool," representing Joseph of Arimathea, an entire suit of Minor Arcana images is used to relate Joseph's role as the "father" of the British church. Next, around each card of the Major Arcana, two cards are presented. For each new milestone of the learner's path, two important lessons had to be learned—most likely one lesson based on Old Testament teachings and one lesson from the New.

After the first set of lessons were learned, Joseph's set, the initiate became a master of that suite—the Cups, the Grail itself. When the next set of lessons were mastered, the set that spoke of Pelagius and the Marian Chalice, he became a master of that set—the pentacles or bowls. He then advanced to the next set, the set of worldly cleanliness, and became a master of the lances or wands. Finally, after mastering the lessons of the swords, he learned the greatest lesson of all—how to stand before the throne of God at Judgment and be deemed clean and pure. This path of the initiate, beginning with a history lesson, leading to a lesson about Pelagius as "an early Cathar," advancing to a lesson on how to lead a pious life, and ending with an outline of the Last Days of the Earth and Christ's return, is depicted below and in the following pages. *(Text follows on page 148.)*

The image of the "Fool" is surrounded by the Ace through the 10 of cups, as well as the Knave, Knight, Queen, and King of cups.

Left to right: Ace of pentacles, The Magician, two of pentacles.

Left to right: three of pentacles, The Popess or Priestess, four of pentacles.

Left to right: five of pentacles, The Empress, six of pentacles.

Left to right: seven of pentacles, The Emperor, eight of pentacles.

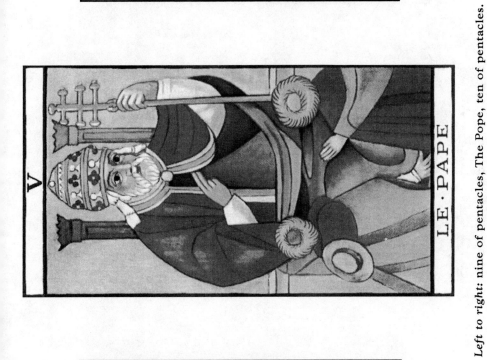

Left to right: nine of pentacles, The Pope, ten of pentacles.

Left to right: Knave of pentacles, The Lovers, Knight of pentacles.

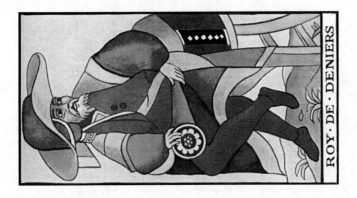

Left to right: Queen of pentacles, The Chariot, King of pentacles.

Left to right: Ace of wands or lances, Justice, two of lances.

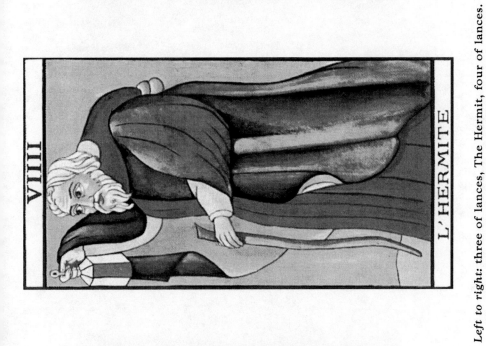

Left to right: three of lances, The Hermit, four of lances.

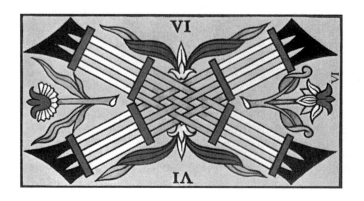

Left to right: five of lances, The Wheel of Fortune, six of lances.

Left to right: seven of lances, Fortitude or Strength, eight of lances.

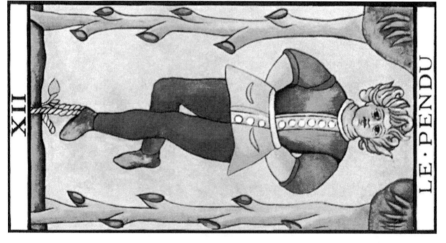

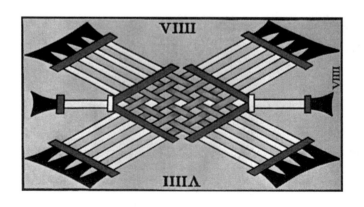

Left to right: nine of lances, The Hanged Man, ten of lances.

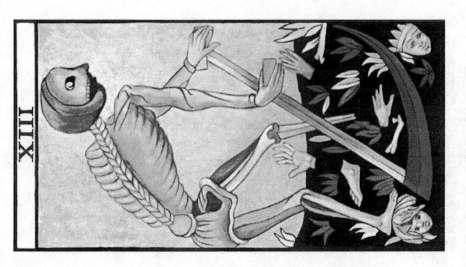

Left to right: Knave of lances, Death, Knight of lances.

ROY·DE·BÂTON

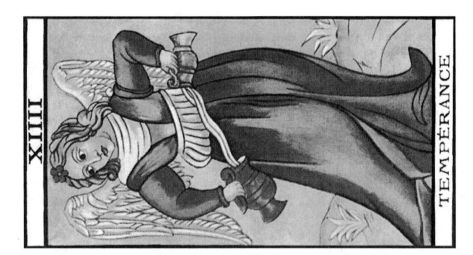

XIIII

TEMPÉRANCE

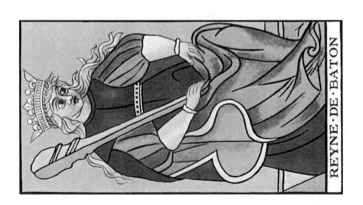

REYNE·DE·BATON

Left to right: Queen of lances, Temperance, King of lances.

Left to right: Ace of swords, The Devil, two of swords.

Left to right: three of swords, The Tower or House of God, four of swords.

Left to right: five of swords, The Star, six of swords.

143

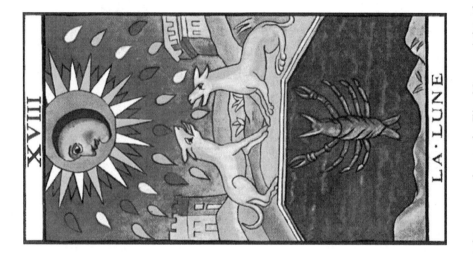

Left to right: seven of swords, The Moon, eight of swords.

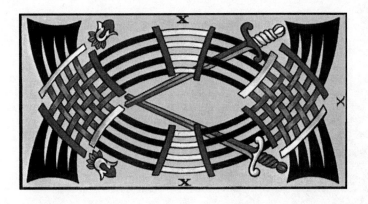

Left to right: nine of swords, The Sun, ten of swords.

CAVALIER·D'ÉPÉE

XX   LE · JUGEMENT

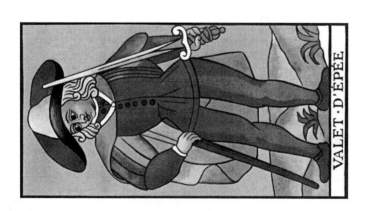

VALET·D'ÉPÉE

Left to right: Knave of swords, Judgment, Knight of swords.

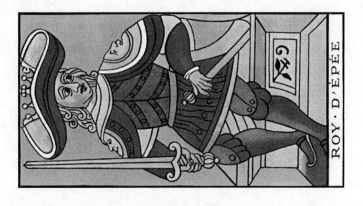

Left to right: Queen of swords, The (New) World, King of swords.

The meaning of the last sequence is quite evident. The progression of the cards from the Major Arcana perfectly matches events as outlined in the Book of Revelation from the *Bible*: Satan is released onto the earth, a burning star descends to earth (destroying the "house of God"—the church) the stars fall from the sky, the moon becomes as blood, the sun becomes black as sack-cloth, the final judgment arrives (with the graves bursting open during the Rapture) and finally comes the descent of the New Jerusalem, the New World. Continuing the theme from the first full set to the last, the second set, associated with the lance, serves as a kind of guide to a clean life on earth while inhabiting a physical body. This set offers the promise of justice for the just, the instruction to lead a solitary, monastic life, how to deal with change, how to maintain your strength when challenged, how to endure trial, how to surpass death, and how to become a temperate being as was Jesus Himself.

Several important aspects of the images seen in the Tarot become visible in this light. Throughout, one can see many instances of light and dark (for example: two columns, one white and the other darker; one figure holding a white sword and another holding a dark sword; etc.). This type of imagery evokes the idea of good and evil, old and new, Mosaic and Christian Laws, etc. Since each image from the Major Arcana is flanked by two from the Minor, this duality becomes all too clear. Similarly, one finds many images of young shoots or buds being cut off, or cut wood revealing a red core. This symbolism possibly references a life cut off in its prime—as was Jesus', or the idea that wood must be young and flexible, rather than old and hardened, to be reshaped.

Several other features point to hidden meanings included in the larger images. For example, the image of the "Popess" is curious in the sense that some versions of the Tarot deck depict her cloak partially obscuring the word "Torah" on the book she holds. This makes perfect sense if this card refers to Helena discovering the tomb of Christ, who was a prophet foretold by the Torah, hidden by a temple dedicated to the goddess Aphrodite. This image is, in fact, one of the most compelling reasons to draw a parallel between the importance of the Old Testament laws and prophecies, and the mysteries surrounding the Pelagians and Cathars.

The image of the Priestess has also been associated with the mythical female pope, Pope Joan Aquila (Joan the Eagle). Here it is important to remember a passage from *La Folie Perceval* in which a woman appears to Perceval in the forest, berating him after his initial failure to ask the appropriate question when he sees the Grail procession. She makes the statement, "I am the eagle who flew higher than any who dwelt in Rome" (Phillips, *The Search for the Grail*, p. 109). Pope Joan is also known for being

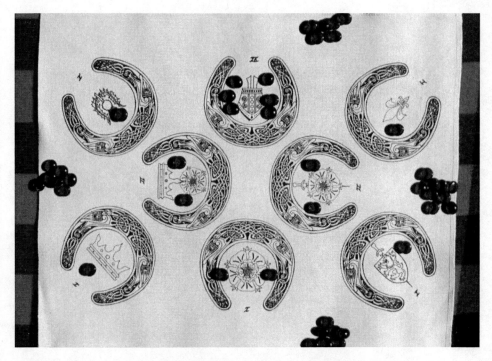

This is a modern recreation of the board game known as "Pope Joan" or, alternately, as "Poch." Historically, the game is played by placing tokens in one of eight "cups." Some versions of this game use a revolving "lazy susan" design, possibly employing actual cups. (Photograph courtesy of Charles Knutson, MacGregor Historic Games.)

the "inspiration" for another game—the "Pope Joan Board." In the game, players try to win tokens kept in eight "bowls." Playing the face cards of the trump suit, the first to get rid of his or her cards wins the hand. The image of eight bowls or other vessels becomes important when one learns that the legend of the Holy Grail might well have been inspired by the histories of seven or eight different "cups."

Other aspects of these images appear symbolic as well, such as the direction faced by each member of the four "court cards" (the Page, Knight, Queen, and King). Also several figures wear the masks of Drama and Comedy on their shoulders. Finally, the Page of Pentacles holds one "bowl" in his hand while a second rests, almost hidden, on the ground by his foot. This is the only one of the Minor Arcana's "court cards" that displays two images of its suit, reflecting the thought that there were, in a sense, two Grails—Joseph's "Grail," which was in fact two small vials, and the Marian Chalice sent from Rome. (In a hidden language of symbols, everything has meaning; nothing is there by chance—including a conspicuous difference between one card and similar cards.) This encrypted book of symbolic meaning, both telling the story of the Grail Hallows and using them as tools for teaching a heretical doctrine, surely played an important role in the creation of the Grail myths as passed down through history. When the West was exposed to other cultures during the Crusades, interest in all things different and mysterious took root in the European mind (even if such interest was forbidden and required the mask of a more accepted guise).

Nearly all early Grail text authors spoke of a sourcebook that could be read only by certain select individuals. To some, the book itself was sacred. To others, it was seen as a book not to be creatively altered, but respectfully retold. In *La Folie Perceval* one sees the closest thing to a direct translation and continuation of this, the earliest written tradition of the relics known as the Grail Hallows.

13

The Grail Hallows

History and legend are usually cast as different characters, at times even as rivals. What many today accept as fact is simply an educated guess substantiated by seemingly credible evidence. The interpretation of this evidence follows the strict guidelines of the scientific method: there is a problem for which one develops a hypothesis, which is then tested, yielding a positive or negative result that either validates or discredits the hypothesis. It seems simple enough; however, the lines between fact and fiction are in truth not so neatly defined.

If historical *fact* and *legend* were portrayed as actors on a stage, *fact* would be the more popular of the two simply because he knows his lines better than *legend*. In other words, both are a retelling of the past, only *fact* has more to say in its favor than does *legend*. That is why legend and folklore have been relegated to the historical equivalent of the doddering old grandfather telling stories by the fireplace to children who do not yet know better. One must remember that the history we rely upon today is present thanks in no small part to oral tradition, or, in other words, to folklore.

When a student of medieval literature or history begins a study of the Grail legend and the legend of the Hallows, that student enters a veritable mine field of intersecting schools of thought. At the same time, one must navigate the tricky waters of religion, history, culture, local folklore, and one's own values. It is necessary to divest oneself of bias and preconception if any sense is to be made of all this conflicting thought. Therefore, such a student or researcher must embark upon his course of learning with the innocence—and, to a degree, ignorance—of a child. To follow a preconceived notion is to force oneself onto what will surely become the wrong path.

With this type of innocent perspective, and the absence of modern-day coloring, one can begin to understand how the legend of the Grail Hallows came into being. Beginning with simple relics that happened to belong to a simple, but monumentally important man, a story was told and retold many, many times, building ever-increasing layers of belief and mysticism centered on these same simple relics. Therefore, when one tries to recreate the mindset held by the people who continued the story, it becomes possible to dissolve each layer, slowly excavating the years of myth and fable, until at last the history that began it all can be seen, shining like a golden coin buried for centuries.

Since the legend of the Grail Hallows is based on a few simple objects, it becomes necessary to understand both these relics from which all the stories sprang, and how these stories became legend. To do this, each relic must be examined in historical context—how it came to be part of Christ's Passion, and what has become of it since. Since the idea of the sourcebook, and its evolution into the modern Tarot deck, has been critical to this investigation of the Grail Hallows, the relics will be examined in similar order—first the two vessels containing the blood of Christ, and then the two weapons—the lance and the sword—that once belonged to two Roman soldiers.

The focus of the Hallows legend is without question the vessel described as the Holy Grail. Although modern retellings of this legend casts the Grail as only one vessel, early versions of the story consider it two at the very least—one chalice that held the blood of Christ, and another said to be a bowl or dish from the upper room that hosted the now famous Last Supper. This should be the first indication to the student of medieval legend that things aren't quite as they would appear. If the Grail is the vessel from the Last Supper, why is another present?

This very paradox leads to a startling conclusion whose impact reaches farther than one would ever expect. The Grail is not simply one object, it is several. According to historical evidence and nearly forgotten tradition, it would seem that the Grail is no less than seven different vessels—two cups or bowls, and five vials, all of which once contained a portion of Christ's blood shed on the cross and in the hastily prepared tomb in which He was sealed. Each of these seven objects contributed to the story of the Grail as we know it today.

The timeline of the Grail can be traced as follows. When Jesus was hung upon the cross, preparations were immediately begun for his burial in a rock-cut tomb. Joseph of Arimathea donated his own tomb to house the body, but he would also donate other grave goods as well. Among these would be a finely woven burial shroud that he most likely acquired during his travels (which included Egypt—the weave closely resembled that used in the wrappings of mummies). Joseph also contributed a fine vessel made of agate, likely obtained in Egypt as well, that was to be used to catch the precious blood that flowed out of the deceased's body. To the Hebrews, the blood was sacred and had to be interred with the body.

This fine agate bowl would later become the relic known as the Santo Caliz of Valencia, Spain (where it resides today). Although it began its life as a simple yet beautiful bowl, it now sits atop an ornate stem, base and handles encrusted with jewels, including rubies and pearls. While it remains unclear whether Chretien wrote his description of the Grail as being encrusted with gold and jewels (the finest from land or sea) before or after this reliquary was built around the agate cup, the Santo Caliz now fits his description perfectly.

It was from this agate bowl that the five vials took their place in legend. After Christ's tomb was found empty, Peter and the others present found this cup in the tomb, still filled with the blood it was meant to contain. From this cup, five vials were filled with a small portion of the blood, and given to Joseph, Nicodemus, and, lastly, Mary Magdalene, whose vials they were. These were, in fact, the remaining five vials from what was originally six, one having been used to anoint Christ's head and feet at the feast in His honor in the house of her sister Martha only days before.

Joseph received two, and took them to Britain to found the Grail legend there at Glastonbury. Two were also given to Nicodemus, the secret follower of Jesus who asked how it was possible to be "born again," saying, "How can a man be born when he is old? Can he enter the second time into his mother's womb, and be born?" (*The Holy Bible*, John 3:4). Nicodemus placed his two vials in a statue of Jesus on the cross that he carved, called the "Volto Santo" or "Holy Face," which can now be found in the town of Lucca, Italy. Finally, since Mary had already used one vial to anoint Jesus, she was given the last one. Interpreted as an "alabaster flask," this vial is called by archeologists an "alabastron," or simply a "perfume vial," which was commonly possessed by women in that time. The "pound of nard" (or spikanard) spoken of in the *Bible* was simply a box containing these six vials of perfumed oil, the weight of their contents being one Hebrew pound, or 12 ounces. It was the remainder of this oil that Jesus told Mary she was to keep and use for his burial.

Although it is impossible to know for sure where these vials came to rest, there are a few popular theories. The two vials brought to England by Joseph of Arimathea were hidden at Glastonbury, found again later, then probably dispersed into the surrounding areas as mentioned in some of the Grail texts, possibly ending up in the hands of the Templars at Roslyn

The Santo Caliz of Valencia, Spain. This is the Eucharist cup that best fits Chretien de Troyes' description of the Grail as being encrusted with the finest gems "in the earth and sea." (Photograph courtesy of Juan C. Gorostizaga, Cofradia del Santo Caliz.)

This ornate unguentarium is one example of the fine quality possible
in even such a simple design. Although this vial is much more decorative than the type Mary possessed when anointing Jesus in the house
of her sister Martha a few days before the Last Supper, the shape and
general design would have been much the same. (Photograph courtesy
of the Frank H. McClung Museum, University of Tennessee.)

Chapel in Scotland or with their modern counterparts in Rome. The two vials that belonged to Nicodemus found their way to Lucca, hidden in the neck of his statue that was sent there for safety, and the vials can now be seen in the town of Luni, Italy, allegedly still containing some of Christ's blood. Finally, the single vial owned by Mary Magdalene found its way to southern France, along with Mary herself, where it likely began the Grail tradition of the Langedoc region made famous by the Cathars and their ill-fated stand at Montsegur.

However, these are not the only relics that played a part in the creation of the modern Grail saga. There still remains one vessel unaccounted for—the bowl from the Last Supper. The early versions of the Grail saga presented the Grail *separate* from this bowl, demonstrating that the early writers differentiated this vessel from the Grail itself. If the notion of the Santo Caliz and the five vials is correct, it still does not account for this bowl. One may then wonder where this tradition originated.

Since the Grail tradition is strongest around Glastonbury (and, in fact, seems to originate from there), it seems likely that the missing piece of this puzzle may be found there as well. There is indeed a tradition, dealing with a bowl found at Glastonbury, that would seem to resolve this issue. In his book *The Search for the Grail*, Graham Phillips speaks of the only known historical mention of a certain relic that could be considered the Grail. He tells the story of Olympiodorus, who wrote in his books of history how Empress Helena Augusta discovered in Christ's tomb a vessel that was thought to have once contained the blood of the crucified Jesus.

Called the "Marian Chalice," this vessel was allegedly taken by Helena back to Rome and presented to her son Constantine the Great as a sacred relic. Some time later, this vessel was sent to Britain for safety during the invasion of Rome in 410. Although Phillips asserts that this vessel was a green onyx vial found in Hawkstone Park in Shropshire, England, it seems more likely that it would have been sent to the only place in England known at the time to possess other blood relics of Christ's Passion—Glastonbury.

There is, in fact, a story surrounding a small, half-destroyed wooden cup from Wales that would seem to corroborate this theory. The Nanteos Cup was allegedly discovered hidden in the walls of Glastonbury Abbey and brought to Strata Florida in Wales, near the present site of the Nanteos Manor house, by several Glastonbury monks who escaped with it before their abbey was dissolved by the king in 1539. Tradition states that this cup was given to the family that would build the manor at Nanteos to guard. In truth, this responsibility is being carried out to this day by the descendents of the Powell family of Nanteos.

This small olive wood bowl is the type of vessel a historian would expect to find at a Hebrew Passover meal such as the Last Supper. It is possible that this bowl was hastily recovered from the upper room that hosted this Passover meal—partly in keeping with the Hebrew tradition that a body was taken to an upper room belonging to a family member to be prepared for placement in the tomb. Since Jesus had no family in the area, this would have been the closest thing to the fulfillment of this tradition. The bowl was then taken to the site of the Crucifixion, where the blood that spilled from the body on the cross was collected. This bowl would have contained not only blood, but the blood-soaked dirt onto which the blood fell. One must remember that the burial ritual required all the blood to be collected and entombed with the body.

This bowl would have joined the fine agate bowl belonging to Joseph that was also left inside the tomb. However, when the tomb was found empty, it would appear that this bowl was left inside, either because it held dirt as well as the blood of Jesus (and so was deemed unsuitable for use as a relic), or to preserve the tradition of leaving the blood of the deceased in the tomb. In either event, this was the only vessel left in the tomb, while its companion, the Santo Caliz, was taken by Peter to Rome. It is this unassuming vessel and its role in the Passover meal that gave rise to the idea that the Grail is a cup from the Last Supper.

If these theories are correct, the Grail tradition at Glastonbury, including the Pelagian heresy, was based first on the two vials Joseph brought with him to Britain, and later on the Marian Chalice, now called the Nanteos Cup, that was sent there by Rome in 410. Although Joseph's vials are now mistakenly interpreted as a chalice in Grail tradition, these two relics are present in the Tarot deck, and certainly in the original sourcebook from which the Tarot evolved over time.

This notion is borne out by the manner in which the Tarot represents these items. While the lance and the sword are depicted in the first card of their suits in the Minor Arcana as being held by a disembodied hand emerging from a cloud, presumably the hand of God, the Grail cup and bowl (represented by the Pentacle) are shown in very earthly, realistic terms. This would seem to indicate that Joseph's Grail and the bowl were in the possession of the Grail devotees that originated the story, while the sword and the lance were not. But if the sword and lance were not included with the relics at Glastonbury, why were they included in the sourcebook detailing their story?

Since what we know of the Grail tradition at Glastonbury fails to provide the answers required, it appears that whoever created the pictorial Grail sourcebook, using the images that would later become the Tarot deck, did so from a perspective somewhat removed from the Glastonbury tradition. Since the trail of the sourcebook and Tarot continuously leads back to the enigmatic medieval heresy known as Catharism, it's logical to conclude that it was the Cathars who added the two other relics to the Grail Hallows, knowing of both relics stories and locations (information unavailable to the inhabitants of sixth-century Glastonbury).

To fully understand how the legend of the Hallows ties in with the history of Glastonbury, the Cathars, and the Tarot, one must carefully consider the way in which the sword and lance are portrayed in the Tarot iconography, as well as the context and time period that would indicate. Therefore, it is necessary to discover when the sword and lance would have become known to the Cathars, as well as any information about why they were depicted as they were in the Tarot. Fortunately, the images found in the mysterious Tarot deck are just enigmatic enough to draw attention to themselves. In investigating the peculiarities of these images, one finds a very clear time period in which the sword and lance would have been portrayed as they were.

The Grail tradition holds that as the feast at the Castle of the Fisher King progresses, a maiden enters with a lance, blood dripping from the tip like a perfect liquid ruby. Some stories view this object with as much reverence as the Grail. Others insist it casts a pall of torment and pain over all present at the feast. It is clear that this is not a simple weapon of war. It is both the instrument of the Fisher King's living death, and a sacred relic.

The spear depicted among the Grail Hallows, whether specifically named or merely implied, is the lance used to pierce Christ's side as He hung on the Cross. Called the "Spear of Destiny" or the "Lance of Longinus," it is simply a Roman spear from the first century. Although it played a particular role in the story of Jesus' crucifixion, one must remember that it belonged to a Roman soldier. Therefore, the question can justifiably be asked, how did it become an object of veneration among Christians?

A Roman soldier from this time period took possession his armaments with the assumption that they were to be returned to a central repository— a storehouse for a specific legion's weapons. For this reason, one may wonder how one lance in particular can be singled out as the spear used to pierce Christ's side. After all, wouldn't it have been returned to the armory and placed alongside all the other lances? Furthermore, how did it ever leave the weapons room at all to become a relic, possessed and venerated throughout Christian Europe?

Although these questions can't be answered with absolute certainty, certain extenuating circumstances may indicate how this Roman weapon came to be in the hands of the yet-to-be-born Christian church. In the book

Matthew in the New Testament, one can read a startling declaration made just after the death of Jesus by none other than one of Jesus' Roman executioners.

> Now when the centurion, and they that were with him, watching Jesus, saw the earthquake, and those things that were done, they feared greatly, saying, Truly this was the Son of God [*The Holy Bible*, Matthew 27:53.

This passage offers a declaration of belief in the holiness of Jesus—made by a Roman soldier, a centurion, at the foot of the Cross. Although this statement falls just short of the Roman declaring himself a follower of Jesus, it demonstrates that at least this one soldier challenged that which he had been told about Jesus, and perhaps became somewhat sympathetic toward the newborn religion.

While this statement remains telling enough, another passage from the *Bible* (again in the book of Matthew) shows a Roman soldier openly admitting he believes in Jesus' holiness when the centurion begs Jesus for help as He comes down out of the Mount of Olives after speaking to the masses that followed Him.

> And when Jesus was entered into Capernaum, there came unto him a centurion, beseeching him, and saying, Lord, my servant lieth at home sick of the palsy, grievously tormented. And Jesus saith unto him, I will come and heal him. The centurion answered and said, Lord, I am not worthy that thou shouldest come under my roof: but speak the word only, and my servant shall be healed. For I am a man under authority, having soldiers under me: and I say to this man, Go, and he goeth; and to another, Come, and he cometh; and to my servant, Do this, and he doeth it. When Jesus heard it, he marvelled, and said to them that followed, Verily I say unto you, I have not found so great faith, no, not in Israel. And I say unto you, That many shall come from the east and west, and shall sit down with Abraham, and Isaac, and Jacob, in the kingdom of heaven. But the children of the kingdom shall be cast out into outer darkness: there shall be weeping and gnashing of teeth. And Jesus said unto the centurion, Go thy way; and as thou hast believed, so be it done unto thee. And his servant was healed in the selfsame hour [*The Holy Bible*, Matthew 8:5–13].

Here a Roman centurion professes his belief in the supernatural powers of Jesus. Without question, if this had been discovered by his superiors, this "man under authority" would have been stripped of that authority, and quite possibly his life. Yet here is a Roman, a pagan, who places his full faith in Jesus in order to heal his servant.

These two passages are important to this study of the Grail Hallows if for no other reason than to demonstrate that it is not impossible, nor too improbable, to believe, that a Roman soldier would provide an object from his armament to the followers of Jesus after His crucifixion. Some of these Roman soldiers may have even set aside their former lives in order to follow Jesus or those who followed Him after His death. Even if this was not the case, it is possible that the owner of that very important lance felt close enough, or fearful enough, to hand his spear over to the Christians, who later placed it in the care of Emperor Constantine, the first Christian Roman Emperor.

The history of this lance throughout medieval Europe is nearly as mysterious and convoluted as the legend of the Grail itself. From its sequestering in Jerusalem after it was allegedly found by Empress Helena in Christ's tomb in 327, it became a trophy object for the kings and sultans of the Eastern World for centuries. Beginning in the early seventh century, the history of the lance reads like the transcript of a football game.

614   Jerusalem is sacked, and the tip of the lance is broken off for safe keeping. When the lance was restored by the Byzantine Emperor Heraclius, the lance's shaft and neck was returned to Jerusalem, while the tip remained in Byzantium.

ca. 775   Charlemagne is given the "Lance of St. Maurice" by the Pope, and later uses it as a symbol of power in A.D. 800.

919   Duke Henry of Saxony is elected King of Germany. Seeking to legitimize his rule, he seeks relics of power, including a lance claimed to be the Lance of Longinus.

962   Pope John XII crowns Henry's son Otto king. As king, Otto makes two copies of the lance passed to him by his father and sends them to the Kings of Hungary and Poland.

994   Otto III ascends to the throne, and further legitimizes his role as the divine ruler by embedding what he claims are nails from the Crucifixion into his lance.

1098   Finally winning their costly victory at Antioch, a soldier claims to have had a vision of St. Andrew in which Andrew showed the soldier where to find the lance of the Crucifixion. They dig where the soldier tells them, and there in the basement of St. Peter's Cathedral they find an ancient lance. This lance's credibility immediately comes into question when the lance is taken to the Emperor, who claims he already has the true lance. At the same time, the Armenian Christians say they possess the true lance. After this, all lances are taken to Constantinople for safety.

1204   Crusaders overrun Constantinople, taking all the lances, as well as a great many other things, as trophies for Baldwin II.

1241   All these relics, including the broken tip to the Lance of Longinus, are sold to King Louis IX of France, where he enshrines them in the newly created reliquary of Sainte Chapelle in Paris. The tip remained there until the French Revolution. The shaft of the lance was returned to Constantinople. The lance of Antioch was lost.

1453   Turks seize Constantinople and take the shaft.

1492   Pope Innocent VIII succeeds in trading the Sultan's imprisoned brother for the lance shaft. The lance was then hidden at the Vatican in one of the four great pillars at St. Peter's Basilica, where it supposedly remains to this day.

1789   French Revolution signals the beginning of the end of the Holy Roman Empire. The broken tip of the lance is taken from the reliquary at Sainte Chapelle to the Bibliotek Nationalle.

1806   The Holy Roman Empire formally disbands, handing over all remnants to the Hapsburg family. The German lance known as the "Lance of St. Maurice" ends up in the Hoffburg Museum in Vienna, Austria.

1938   Inspired by Wagner's opera *Parzifal*, the charismatic new leader of the German people, Adolph Hitler, takes the lance from the Hoffburg museum, again to use as a magical talisman of power.

1945   After Hitler's death, General Mark Clark discovers the lance. It is returned to the Hoffburg Museum in January of 1946, where it remains today.

Today   The shaft remains in the Vatican Pillar. A copy of Otto's lance remains in Krakow, Poland. The Armenian lance remains a cultural treasure there. The lances of Antioch and Constantine have been lost.

Much like the stories of pieces of the True Cross floating around medieval Europe, tales of the Lance have been a part of European lore since the time of Christ. However, its curious past does nothing to explain how it came to be included in the legends of the Grail Hallows. To find an answer to this question, one must again look back to the origins of the legend.

If one examines the Tarot deck and the four suits of the Major Arcana, it seems clear that the four Grail Hallows are somehow tied in with the cards' creation. Furthermore, when one realizes that the suit meant to represent the lance, the wands, is represented simply as a wooden staff, one may therefore assume that the lance to which the Tarot creators were referring was the lance in the form of the shaft alone, albeit the shaft from the one true lance.

The shaft of the lance was well known in Jerusalem from the time of its recovery by Heraclius after the 614 sacking of Jerusalem until it was taken to Constantinople in 1098. Removed from Constantinople in 1204, it was sold to King Louis IX of France nearly forty years later. After that, the lance was again returned to Constantinople, taken by the Turks, recovered by the Pope, and finally came to rest at the Vatican in one of the pillars in the great Cathedral of St. Peter's in 1492. The longest period of time it remained in one place, and in relative safety, was between 614 and 1098.

The history of the lance, as well as this very specific time period, highlights another interesting aspect of the Hallows legend. The lance found in the Hoffberg museum in Vienna is said to be the lance head from the one true lance. However, someone examining this peculiar relic would not at first think it looked much like a spear. It looks more like a sword— specifically, an early Roman Gladius from the first century A.D. Since a sword of this time period is included among the Grail Hallows was this seen as the sword that beheaded John the Baptist, rather than the Lance of Longinus?

Without a doubt, the sword is the most mysterious and problematic of all the Hallows. Little is known about it, there is no historical record of it, and, other than the account in the *Bible*, there is no evidence at all that it ever existed. Yet somehow it came to be included among the relics that are otherwise associated with the death of Jesus, not with John the Baptist. Why was it included in this auspicious grouping of religious relics, in the Grail texts, and in the Tarot imagery?

It seems that mystery and questions without answers often lead to discovery. And it is no different with the sword. The fact that so little is known about it, and that it doesn't appear in history, leads the historical investigator to one simple yet astounding conclusion. It *didn't* exist—at least not as the legend of the Grail Hallows would have it appear. In fact, as has been mentioned previously, the author himself mistakenly concluded that the artifact in the Hoffberg museum is the sword that beheaded John the Baptist, thinking that the only reason it was included among the Grail Hallows is that it was truly a sword, *the* sword in fact that had been incorrectly identified as a lance head.

This is not the first time this mistake was made. This relic has been misinterpreted as the sword that beheaded John the Baptist for reasons other than its resemblance to a type of sword used during this time period. There already existed a tradition involving this artifact, one well known to the Cathars (who appear to have created the Tarot imagery, as well as the pictorial sourcebook from which at least some of the early Grail texts were taken).

Since the Cathars appear to have been influenced by the much earlier Pelagian tradition in Britain, they likely read the writings of these early heretics,

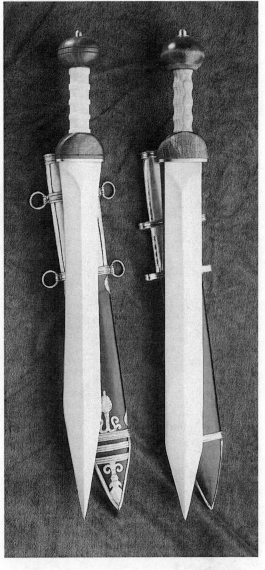

The Roman short sword called the gladius was a weapon commonly found in the Roman military. The example shown on the left is an older gladius, more like what one might find on a first-century Roman soldier, while the example on the right is from somewhat later. Note the gentle narrowing of the blade in the middle section of the sword on the first-century model. This shape looks quite like that of the "Spear of Destiny" found in the Hoffburg Museum. (Photograph by Danny Lee, courtesy of Terry Moss, Museum Replicas, a division of Atlanta Cutlery.)

including the story of Christ's Passion and the Grail's coming to Britain. Because this story was written by Pelagians (a group of people who valued the Mosaic teaching of the Old Testament as much as the New Testament) about early Christians who still maintained Hebrew traditions, it is likely that the tale of John the Baptist would have been included as a very important part of this story.

John is said to be the last prophet of the Old Testament, as well as the precursor to the coming of Jesus. Therefore, his story would have been inexorably intertwined with that of Jesus, especially if the story were told by Joseph of Arimathea, who must be considered a Hebrew despite his following of and association with Jesus. Christianity, as an organized faith, did not come along until some time later, and then in a different part of the world. It must have been for this reason that the story of John the Baptist—and that of his own relic, the sword—was told alongside the tale of Joseph bringing Christ's blood to Britain.

Centuries later when the Cathars co-opted this story, as

This image of the Roman Centurion is quite like what would have been seen at the foot of the cross during Christ's crucifixion. Note that this soldier holds a pilum—a long, thin lance common in the first century. It most likely would have been this type of lance that was used to pierce Christ's side as He hung on the cross. (Photograph by Don Contreras, courtesy of Terry Moss, Museum Replicas, a division of Atlanta Cutlery.)

Labeled the "Spear of Destiny," this lance point has also been called the Lance of Longinus—the spear that pierced Christ's side during the Crucifixion. Although scholars agree that this is simply a lugged spear with dagger blades attached to both sides of the blade's lower half, the idea of this spear as a holy relic had an impact on medieval history, and was held by many of the Holy Roman Empire's greatest emperors. It is curious that this spear is separated into two halves, giving the appearance of the blade having been "broken." The spear's resemblance to an early Roman gladius may have caused some to believe that this spear was instead the sword that beheaded John the Baptist, casting it in Grail lore as a mystical sword that only breaks under special conditions. The image of a broken sword appears repeatedly throughout Grail and Cathar symbology. (Photograph courtesy of Benedikt Haupt, Kunsthistorisches Museum, Vienna.)

recorded by Blaise at the behest of Merlin, they read about the sword as well as the lance, the cup, and the bowl, and then included them in their own teachings and doctrine (as the painting at Montreal de SOS would indicate). However, since they were not as familiar, nor as contemporaneous, with the story and the relics in Britain as were the Pelagians, they made a simple but very important mistake. The Cathars read about these other relics and assumed that they were part of the "relic horde" at

Glastonbury, or at least that they had originally been kept all together, perhaps in the reliquary storehouses of Constantinople.

It is at this point that time plays a critical role in understanding the Cathars' involvement with, and conception of, the lance and the sword, as well as why they were included in the Tarot images. The lance, in the form of the shaft and neck, could be found in Jerusalem from the time just after the sacking of Jerusalem in 614 until it was removed to Constantinople in 1098. Here is five hundred years during which time the lance's shaft, and perhaps part of the head, was well known.

Similarly, the spearhead now housed in Austria makes an appearance in history during this time period. Charlemagne is given this lance by the pope in 775; and then in 994, Otto III obtains the same lance, and embeds in its blade what he claims are nails from the Crucifixion. Although this is still quite a broad time frame at just over two hundred years, it does provide an important link to the Cathar movement. It is just after Otto's ascent to the throne and his act of placing nails in his lance that history sees the first clear signs of the Cathar doctrine, around the year 1000.

Recalling that the sword, whether mentioned in the Grail texts, shown in the Tarot, or seen on the cave wall at Montreal de SOS, is usually shown as broken, one must consider a connection between it and the Austrian lance, which is similarly divided into two halves. The only question that remains is when this divided lance might have been seen by religious pilgrims and other onlookers. Since the copies Otto III had made and sent to the kings of Poland and Hungary also show the lance as being divided, one can assume that it was separated into two pieces some time between Charlemagne's reign and the beginning of Otto's rule.

The Austrian lance has also been called the sword of St. Maurice, named after a famous Roman soldier who became a martyr and a saint. Therefore, it seems likely that the Cathars who created the pictorial source-book outlining what they thought was the full history of the Grail, the bowl, the lance in Jerusalem, and the sword, saw this relic around the year 1000 and assumed they had completed the puzzle. There lay the sword, a Roman sword that had become a powerful religious relic, which could only be the sword that had beheaded John the Baptist, the one the early writings from the Pelagians in Britain seemed to mention.

Now it would appear that all the Grail Hallows are present and accounted for. The original Grail cup had been mistaken for the two vials brought to Britain by Joseph, as well as the other vials which were their mates. The bowl from the Last Supper had been found by Helena, sent to Joseph's church in Britain around the time of the Pelagian heresy, and sent later to Wales. The lance sat safely in Jerusalem, was conveyed to

Constantinople around the same time as the rise of the Cathar movement, and is now at the Vatican (hidden in one of the Pillars at St. Peter's Basilica). Finally, the sword remains a lost relic of man's attempt to understand the past. Most importantly, these relics have come down to us today through history thanks largely to two separate heresies—and one misused and misunderstood deck of cards.

14

An Altered Perspective

The Merriam-Webster Dictionary defines history as "a branch of knowledge that records and explains past events." However, it also defines it as "an established record." These may not at first appear to be two contradictory statements, but as any student of history or archeology would admit, history is still what we make of it. As learned and well versed as a scholar may be, if that individual was not present as history unfolded, there is no way of truly knowing if one's suppositions are completely accurate.

For example, if an archeologist digs in the rich soil of England and finds a wedge-shaped piece of bronze, he or she may conclude it is the blade of some woodworking implement, perhaps an adze or a carving tool. This is mere supposition, however. If the archeologist was not there hundreds or thousands of years before to observe this tool being used, and by whom, there is no way to say for certain what its use really was.

Yet, to put it simply, there history is. We have a history of the world as archeologists and historians have written it down for centuries. Should all history books therefore be considered works of fiction—a fun but weighty read, and ultimately of no consequence? Of course not. Science and further archeology indicate that these "educated guesses" made by archeologists and historians are usually right on the mark. However, one must realize that anything that comes from a person's mind, or the collaborative minds of several, is still just theory. They may be very good theories, they may even be completely accurate, but one must admit that they may also be inherently flawed, and may even become downright ridiculous over the course of time.

The point is, to investigate a "legend" (defined by Merriam-Webster as "a story coming down from the past; *especially*: one popularly regarded as historical although not verifiable") is far from an act of sheer folly. It is—and should ever be considered as—a valid study in, and of, history. One should refrain from dismissing legend as merely an ancient ignorance, because all history is, in fact, legend, albeit to a lesser degree. Some would argue that the line is not so blurred as it would seem here, because "accepted" history is substantiated by historical reference and writing. Although this still falls short of indisputable proof, most accept it as evidence good enough to reclassify theory as fact.

The legend of the Grail Hallows is backed by historical reference and writing. The articles that compose the Grail Procession—the cup, the bowl, the spear, and the sword—have all been mentioned in history, and have appeared many times in several different written forms, not all of them penned by medieval storytellers. What makes these objects the subject of legend rather than accepted history is that much of their story comes from an oral tradition and folklore. Although some maintain that this is inadequate as historical evidence, one must remember that much of our own western culture and history originated with the same type of oral tradition.

Legend states that Rome was founded by the abandoned brothers Romulus and Remus. Their story is fantastic—surely not historical in any way. However, while the story of these founding fathers of Rome being reared by a she-wolf and a woodpecker sounds unlikely, it cannot be said that the legend is "unhistorical." Undoubtedly there is some historical truth in the story of two brothers (whether actually called "Romulus" and "Remus" or not) who played an important role in the founding of Rome. Therefore, we cannot say that this legendary story is entirely unhistorical.

It is similarly impossible to state that the Grail Hallows, relics of a first-century crucifixion, are not historical. However, no one can justly say that their tale is entirely true either. The truth is often found somewhere between two extremes—the Grail Hallows story is not as medieval literature maintains, but the relics themselves most likely did exist, possibly surviving to medieval times or even the modern day. Therefore, all one can do is examine the historical references available, consider the Hallows in light of what has been written (along with what the oral tradition claims), and attempt to separate their history from their fiction.

To begin this process, it was necessary to look back to the foundation of these relics and their stories. All these objects entered history *and* legend at the time of the Crucifixion, with the conspicuous exception of one— the sword. This one artifact, curiously associated with a contemporary of Jesus but not Jesus Himself, was included alongside its more well-known counterparts in the Grail Procession, and appeared to have equal significance. This is the first indication to the historical researcher of a much deeper and more complex mystery.

Then the path of research leads beyond the land of the Crucifixion, and enters the foggy realm where history and legend merge. From the historical facts, two separate traditions emerge. On one side is the Christian history that follows the course taken by Joseph of Arimathea to Britain after the death of Jesus. On the other side is the Celtic branch of the story that most scholars believe suitably explains the origin of the Grail Hallows as a Christianized plagiarism of Celtic mythology.

It is along this latter path that the researcher must first travel to determine if there is any historical truth to the legend at all. It becomes very clear very quickly why scholars assert that the Grail and its associated relics were simply the creation of Celtic lore taken by Christian European writers and altered slightly to suit their audience. Celtic mythology includes magical cauldrons, enchanted spears, and fickle swords that both serve and fail their wielders. Similarly, one can see the character of King Arthur in classically Celtic texts, riding into the Celtic underworld to recover the cauldron of rebirth and the cornucopia of plenty. There seems to be no question as to the Grail's Celtic origin.

However, history is a vast and complex subject, and it must be swept thoroughly using both a broad and fine-toothed comb. An accepted historical writer, Olympiodorus, makes reference to a cup or similar vessel found by Empress Helena Augusta in the tomb that has been widely accepted as that in which Christ's body was laid. Olympiodorus recorded that a vessel, called the "Marian Chalice," was taken to Rome, only to be sent away from the city in 410 for its protection during barbarian attacks.

This historical reference seems at odds with the accepted explanation of the Hallows' history. Although this alone is not enough to completely debunk the Celtic theory, the reference, coupled with the fact that relics from the Roman period have not only been recovered, but recovered by the hundreds of thousands, makes the concept that these religious objects are actual archeological artifacts far from inconceivable. However, such a strong tie to Celtic tradition is not to be ignored, regardless of this historical reference. One must wonder why such similar items appear in both historical records and Celtic mythology.

The Hallows, as represented in Celtic tradition, were but four among the objects known as the Treasures of Britain, belonging to the legendary Tuatha de Danaan. The story of the Tuatha, like the legend of the Hallows, is one that seems to mate history with fantasy. These people, called the

"Faery Folk" and "the Shining Ones," were said to have come with their magical relics from lands to the north out of a magical bank of fog. They came first to Scotland, later traveling into Ireland and further into England, the fog from whence they came most likely being the smoke from their own burning boats.

To one familiar with the history of ancient Britain, the story of the Tuatha de Danaan sounds a great deal like the arrival of the Anglo-Saxons on British shores from the Norse lands to the north. While the legends of fair, shining, fairy-like people do not immediately evoke the image of a fierce warrior from the land of the Vikings, the student of history should remember that, along with foreign warriors, invasion brings different cultures that sometimes replace, but more often mingle with, the native cultures of those being invaded.

With this in mind, one can easily see the Anglo-Saxon influence in such traditionally Celtic icons as the Book of Kells, filled with snarling dragon-like animals and stylized human figures. The images from this book very closely resemble the carvings on the mastheads of Viking longboats recovered from the archeological record over the past hundred years. Furthermore, the act of ritually burning boats is witnessed in the Anglo-Saxon saga of Beowulf. Therefore, one may wonder if the legendary Tuatha de Danaan came to Britain not in body, but in the traditions of the invading Anglo-Saxons. If this was the case, how did the story of the Tuatha become tied to the legend of Christian relics housed in Britain?

One other theory about the origins of the Tuatha in Britain stems from a controversial concept regarding the 12 Tribes of Israel. From the original 12 tribes, 10 were said to have become lost to history, among which was the Tribe of Dan. Some historical evidence suggests that this group traveled throughout the Mediterranean, visiting the Greeks and many other peoples of the time. Eventually, they are said to have come to Denmark, also called Daanmark, which has been translated as "the Land of Daan" in reference to the Tribe of Dan. Scotland's constitution also makes reference to their own tradition that they had been founded by one of the Tribes of Israel.

Regardless of one's views on the subject, one must consider the notion that in this area of the world, at this time, there was a tradition that a lost Israelite group, known as the Daan, were present in Britain (whether that concept came from the invading Anglo-Saxons or was already ensconced when they arrived). Therefore, if the Anglo-Saxon invaders happened to find in Britain a group who claimed to be descended from people originally native to Israel, this surely would have stirred the legend of the Daan in Britain (or even might have been its origin).

But what are the chances that the Tuatha de Danaan legend was based on a lost group of Israelite descendants living in Britain? Actually, the chances might be quite good indeed. If one accepts the story of Joseph of Arimathea founding the original wattle church at Glastonbury, it follows that the descendants of his original followers would have remained there to look after Joseph's church, and would be familiar with the story of how they came to Britain. Therefore, it seems quite possible that the tradition of the Tuatha de Danaan as the holders of the Treasures of Britain was somehow influenced by, mixed with, or possibly even originated by the tradition of relics being held at Glastonbury by those who came after Joseph and his contemporaries.

Another aspect of the "Tribe of Dan" legend may have perpetuated this idea. One name ascribed to this lost tribe during their time with the Greeks was "the Pelasgians." In the decades just before the Anglo-Saxon invasion in 450, a man by the name of Pelagius left Britain to suggest to the church in Rome that the church in Britain should be recognized as a legitimate branch of the Christian faith because of their apostolic succession (via a direct disciple of Jesus—Joseph of Arimathea). Furthermore, the British sect held sacred relics of Christ's Passion that legitimized their right to this title. But Rome saw the issue differently.

Ultimately, the Pelagian movement was called a heresy, and all who followed it were excommunicated by the Roman church. Now called the "Pelagians," those who held with the tradition of Joseph's church in Britain were considered outcasts, but likely maintained their own beliefs. Around this time, the "Marian Chalice" was sent to Britain by its keepers in Rome, surely reassuring the followers of the British church that they were not completely forgotten, both by God and by the roots of the original Christian Church. A relatively short time later, the period ascribed to King Arthur gave rise to another enigmatic man called Merlin, who, according to several texts, narrated the first account of the Grail's history to his mother's confessor priest, Blaise (also called Blayse, Blois, etc.).

Although the character of Merlin is possibly the most difficult to consider in terms of a true historical figure, Norma Lorre Goodrich and other Arthurian researchers believe the character of Merlin to be based not only on one historical individual, but on two different men whose lives blended together to create the popular image of Merlin as a dark, magical figure who served Arthur (and who became a "wild man of the forest" in later years). Again working from the assumption that every legend has at its root a grain of truth, if there was a historical Merlin living during the time of the Pelagians, then he would have been able to preserve their tradition and that of the Glastonbury church in a book, as is suggested by works such as *The Prose Merlin*.

This book, narrated by Merlin and penned by Blaise, would not only have outlined the history of the Grail, but all the relics housed at Glastonbury, as well as the story of how they came there, the story of Joseph's church, and the story of the events surrounding the Crucifixion itself. For those who lived and worked at the church to maintain its traditions and guard its relics, this was the book of their history. Although there is no way to know exactly what the book contained, it seems logical to think that this book was lengthy, detailing all the exploits of Joseph and his followers who brought the original relics to Britain some five hundred years before. Like most books of the period, it most likely would have included beautifully created pictures and illuminations that assisted in the telling of the story, perhaps for those in the community who were not literate.

It would also stand to reason that if Merlin and Blaise thought it necessary to write the history of the relics housed at Glastonbury, they would have included the story of its greatest contemporary proponent—the heretic Pelagius. Since he had returned to Britain not only with the news of his failure, but seemingly with another relic of Christ's Passion, this book surely would have included (and possibly even been inspired by) the story of his epic trip to Rome, his return in defeat, and the arrival of the second relic at Glastonbury. Thus, the first book of the Grail Hallows would have been a history of the relics housed at Glastonbury, most likely ending with the story of Pelagius and the arrival of the Marian Chalice. However, the story doesn't end here. The book was picked up again by a later, but like-minded group.

Similarly called "heretics," the medieval group of lay-monks called Cathars became a part of the Grail legend when they too claimed to possess the one true Grail. The tale becomes all the more poignant when one reads about the end of their order on the rocky slopes of Montsegur in southern France. The story claims that as their fortress lay besieged, a small number of their order escaped the mountaintop stronghold with something of great importance to their brotherhood. Although it remains unclear exactly what was spirited away before the rest of their order was burned at the stake, it is surmised that it was either texts of great importance to their order, or even their Grail itself.

Many tell-tale signs of Catharism can be found in the area, with none so intriguing as a cave painting below the castle ruins at Montreal de SOS. Still visible, although worn by the ravages of time, this painting shows some very familiar items as being important to the Cathars—a lance; a sword that reportedly was originally depicted as broken; a "disk" that could be interpreted as a shining bowl or dish; and, in a much more cryptic form, a "Grail" in the sense of an apparently important object containing drops of blood and marked with crosses—the reverential signs of holiness.

This and other such depictions in the area are more than just interesting archeological "doodles." These images appear to have been used as part of an initiation rite during the process of becoming a Cathar, or as part of their learning catechism. The lance, the sword, the dish or bowl, and a holy relic that has been called the Grail seem to have been central to their teachings, and of great importance to their faith. Although it does not appear that the Cathars possessed all of these relics, whether they held a Grail or not, they were familiar with these artifacts and their stories.

The cave painting not only demonstrates the Cathars' familiarity with the relics, it provides an important link to the further understanding of the Hallows legend. Although it is currently unclear whether or not the painting depicted the sword as being broken, the image of a broken sword does continuously reappear both in Grail literature and in imagery associated with it and the other Hallows. Nearly every text dealing with the Hallows includes a magical sword. It is a weapon that will protect its holder until the moment of dire need (or a similarly "preordained" circumstance).

The sword, along with its fellow Hallows, also appears in the deck of cards called the Tarot. The four suits in the "Minor Arcana" (the cards that closely resemble a modern deck of playing cards) are, in fact, the sword, the lance, and the Grail cup and bowl. This alone would suggest that the Tarot deck had its origins with the Cathar movement. Although this curious deck of cards is thought to have first appeared in 1441, similar types of card decks have been described in 1392 (in the court of King Charles VI of France), and even earlier, back to the same time as the foundation of the Cathar movement.

The broken sword also appears in the "Major Arcana," or picture cards of the Tarot deck. Although an intact sword is held in the right hand of the lady on the "Justice" card, a broken sword blade can be seen in the left hand on the "Devil" card. It would appear that the creators of the Tarot deck were familiar not only with the sword from the Hallows, but specifically a *broken* sword. Someone living during the time of the Cathars might have thought just such a sword existed in the treasury of the Germanic King Otto. Otto possessed—and made copies of—a relic that, although he claimed it was the lance from the Crucifixion, gave every appearance of being a Roman gladius sword from the first century.

The appearance of this relic may have reminded the early Cathars of the stories about John the Baptist and the sword that beheaded him, especially if they possessed the texts and early writings of the Pelagians, who apparently influenced the Cathar doctrine. Judging by the images from the first third of the Tarot's Major Arcana, it would seem that the Cathars not only knew the stories of the four relics, but the history of Joseph at Britain and of Pelagius as well. One can see what might have been the Blaise manuscript presented in pictorial form in the Major Arcana cards "the Fool" (representing Joseph's arrival in Britain), and cards one through seven (representing Merlin's dictation of the Grail story all the way through the arrival of the Marian Chalice in Britain).

Apart from these images derived from the Blaise text, what of the remainder of the Tarot deck—the Major Arcana cards eight through 21, and the Minor Arcana? Considering the scenes depicted in the rest of the Major Arcana, one can easily get the impression that they serve to teach a lesson. The second third of the Major Arcana cards speak of justice, fortitude, temperance and death, as well as earthly concerns such as solitude, the turn of fate, and trial by one's fellow man.

The meaning of the deck's final third seems clear. It retraces, almost exactly, the story of the Apocalypse as read from the *Bible*'s book of Revelation. Beginning with the release of the Devil onto the earth and the end of God's church, it proceeds through the signs that tell of approaching Armageddon, and ends with God's judgment and the coming of the New Earth.

The images in the Major Arcana suggest a type of guidebook or teaching tool for the initiate on how to lead a proper life, as well as offering knowledge of the past, so that when one stands before God he or she will be deemed worthy. So what might be the meaning of the Minor Arcana? This is much more difficult to determine. If paired with the cards from the Major Arcana, one on both sides of each Major Arcana card, an added dimension develops in this "guidebook," giving it the appearance of an indepth teaching guide or learning tool used to usher a new initiate into the Cathar doctrine through a vast sacrament of learning and purification on his way to becoming a perfect servant of God.

If this "guidebook" was the earliest form of the Grail Hallows legend, one might wonder if it was also the source of the legend as written today. Since this Cathar "picture book" that has since become the Tarot deck included the original story as written by Blaise about the history of the Grail relics, this would make sense, especially if one remembers the little-known Grail text entitled *La Folie Perceval*, in which the characters of the story seem to follow the progression of images shown in the Major Arcana. However, how does one explain the role played by the rest of the Cathar picture book in the context of the Grail saga?

While the beginning of the story seems fairly standard (a youth, ignorant of the ways of knighthood, finds his way to Arthur's court and then later to the castle of the Fisher King and the Grail procession), the events after his initial encounter vary, his course twisting and winding along an uncertain path that later appears to carry some mystical meaning. In this respect, the story of Perceval, the original Grail hero, does seem to follow the notion of one who is unlearned being introduced to something greater than himself, and then traveling the long and arduous path toward understanding.

Therefore, it would appear that the texts dealing with the Grail and the Hallows written in medieval times did indeed come from a sourcebook, just as the authors Chretien de Troyes and Wolfram von Eschenbach claimed. However, there is still the unresolved issue of the Celtic branch of the Grail legend. There does appear to be very close ties between the Celtic tradition and the origins of the early Grail texts. Though on the surface this seems to be a considerable paradox, in truth it really doesn't present that great a problem. If one assumes Joseph did indeed come to Britain to start his church with his relics from the Holy Land and the Crucifixion, and that Blaise did indeed write the first chronicle of the relics at Glastonbury (including the story of Pelagius and the coming of the second relic from Rome), it then becomes clear that the Grail tradition at Glastonbury might well have influenced Celtic tradition with regard to their own mythology surrounding such sacred or "magical" objects, resulting in a "Celtic branch" of the Grail story. If there were two "Merlins," as Goodrich claims, the Merlin that has been called the "wild man of the forest" might even have taken the Glastonbury story to the Celtic people, thinking himself the same as the Merlin who first narrated the story to Blaise.

If the Blaise text found its way to the Celts, resulting in the more Celtic versions of the story (such as *Peredur*), this may explain why the early parts of both stories are so similar (the story of how Perceval becomes a knight and goes to the castle of the Fisher King), but diverge in focus after that. If the sourcebook that informed the first part of *Peredur* was the same as that used by Chretien, both authors would have needed to find additional material for the remainder of the text—Chretien possibly using a more text-based version of the Cathar manuscript as a guide, while the Celtic author employed the mythology of his own culture.

In the end, it is impossible to say whether or not the Grail texts were created in this manner, just as it is impossible to say for certain whether or not the Grail Hallows ever existed at all. However, the historical references, textual references, and common use of similar imagery in apparently non-related sources would suggest that these holy objects did, in fact, exist as archeological relics. It would appear that these artifacts of the Crucifixion began a tradition of relic keeping and sacredness that had affected history from the time of their creation until now. Touching many separate traditions, ranging from the British church and the Pelagian heresy, to Catharism and the mystical Tarot deck, the Grail Hallows have survived the unkind hand of opposition and the ever-changing nuances of the human condition to pique our curiosity and beg us to question—just as it was intended to do when the legend was born two thousand years ago.

To the reader goes this final admonishment. When you next sit down with a deck of playing cards for a peaceful game of solitaire or a lively game of poker, take a moment to look at the simple paper cards in your hand. Take time to examine the faces of the King, the Queen, and the Jack. Ponder the club, the diamond, the spade, and the heart. Remain still and silent, and think of the Grail Hallows. Perhaps you will hear the eternal voice once again ask the question, "What is the Grail and whom does it serve?" If you are fortunate, and if you carefully consider all that has been presented herein, you might be better equipped to answer, and receive your reward thanks in no small part to the cards you hold—still alive today, born from the blood of Jesus Christ.

Appendix:
Timeline, 2500 Years,
from the Reign of Solomon
to the Dissolution of
the Monasteries in Great Britain

970–928 B.C.	Solomon reigns as king of Israel. It was during this time that he built the famous Temple of Solomon.
ca. 926 B.C.	The 12 Tribes of Israel split in two, creating the 10 tribes that would later be considered "lost" to history.
5 B.C.–A.D. 3	Jesus is born in Bethlehem to Mary and Joseph. About six months before His birth, John the Baptist, known as the "Precursor," is born to Mary's cousin, Elizabeth, and her husband Zachary.
ca. A.D. 30	John the Baptist is beheaded by order of King Herod after John accused the king of adultery.
ca. 35	Jesus is crucified and entombed with a number of relics. It is at this point that the relics ascribed to His Passion become the object of legend.
45–80	Joseph of Arimathea arrives in Britain with two cruets containing relics of Christ's blood and sweat at what is now the site of Glastonbury Abbey.

80–100	Joseph's wattle church is erected at Glastonbury on the current site of the Lady Chapel.
135	Roman Emperor Hadrian seeks to destroy all sacred artifacts. Christian persecution begins.
250–260	Helena, future mother of Constantine the Great, is born in Bithynia in Asia Minor.
270	Helena marries Roman general Constantius Chlorus.
293	Constantius divorces Helena to marry co-emperor Maximian's step-daughter.
312	Constantine becomes Emperor after the battle of Milvian Bridge. He declares Christianity the official religion of the empire.
327	Helena allegedly discovers Christ's tomb in Jerusalem. In it, she finds many artifacts of Christ's Passion, including three crosses (or segments thereof), nails, and other artifacts, most importantly the Marian Chalice.
327–336	Helena "parades" cross and other relics throughout the Welsh countryside.
336	Helena dies in Nicomedia in Asia Minor.
380	British monk Pelagius leaves Britain for Rome to confront the Pope regarding the status of the British Church as another "official" church, descended, he claimed, from another apostolic line of succession.
380	The "Gospel of Nicodemus" or "Acts of Pilate" is first clearly mentioned, including the story of Longinus and his spear.
410	Alaric sacks Rome, and the Marian Chalice is sent to Britain for safety. Pelagius leaves Rome for Africa.
416	The Roman Church declares the teachings of Pelagius and his followers a heresy, and all are excommunicated.
443–461	St. Patrick travels to Britain to find the community at Glastonbury and the early wattle church in a state of disarray. This is the most likely date for the covering of lead and boards to have been erected around the wattle church for its protection.

449	Angles, Saxons and Jutes begin invading Britain.
450	In a text associated with Maelgwn (Melkin), who describes himself as being "before Merlin," Melkin states, "Joseph of Arimathea, the noble decurion, received his everlasting rest with his eleven associates in the Isle of Avalon. He lies in the Southern angle of the bifurcated line of the Oratorium of the Adorable Virgin. He has with him the two white vessels of silver which were filled with the blood and the sweat of the great Prophet Jesus."
450	According to Norma Lorre Goodrich, "Merlin One," whom Geoffrey of Monmouth calls "Merlinus," is born.
6th century	A man named Antonius sees the Holy Lance while on a pilgrimage to Jerusalem.
536	"Merlin One" dies.
552	King Arthur dies after the battle of Camlaan.
573	The Battle of Ardderyd (Arthuret) occurs. According to Goodrich, "Merlin Two," who is called "Myrddin Wilt" or "Merlin the Wild," goes mad and retreats into the woods, becoming a Druidic priest.
591	The first historical indications of a Cathar-like doctrine.
614	Jerusalem is sacked. The tip of the Holy Lance is broken off for safety. After Emperor Heraclius recovered the lance, the tip went to the Chapel of Pharos in Constantinople, and the shaft and neck of the spear went to Jerusalem.
712	King Ine builds his addition to the Olde Chirche at Glastonbury.
713	The Santo Caliz is conveyed to a safe hiding place in a cave at the Huesca monastery.
720	In an account bearing a striking resemblance to that of Melkin's, a story appears of a "certain hermit of Britain" having a vision or dream of an angel who tells him the location of Joseph's tomb at Glastonbury, as well as that of his relics. This account was allegedly written in a text called "Of the Grail" or "de Gradale."

742	The wooden statue called the Volto Santo, said to have been carved by Nicodemus himself, arrives in Lucca, Italy, and is found to contain two vials of blood relics hidden inside the head in the area of the neck.
744	Further indications of a Cathar-like doctrine are seen.
775	The Pope gives Charlemagne the Lance of St. Maurice, which was said to have been used by Constantine to draw the boundaries of Constantinople. Despite its alleged antiquity, this spear had a very seventh-century look.
800	Charlemagne crowns himself emperor.
854	Joan Aquilla (the Eagle) becomes Pope. Legend states that Pope Joan was a woman disguised as a man whose secret was only uncovered when she gave birth while riding a horse after having an affair with a local bishop. A character in the medieval French manuscript *La Folie Perceval* is said to be based on this legendary figure—a wise woman in the forest who claimed she had "flown higher than any Pope in Rome."
962	Otto I becomes emperor of the Holy Roman Empire. The supposed lance head known as the "Spear of Destiny" housed in the Hoffburg Museum in Austria fell into his hands, and is likely found in two pieces at this time.
1000–1022	Further growth of early Cathar doctrine.
1024	Emperor Otto III commissions two copies of the lance to be made. He sends one copy to the king of Poland, and the other to the king of Hungary. In both copies, the lance is made in two pieces.
1025	A group sounding much like the Cathars appears in the Arras region, abstaining from sexual intercourse for reasons of ritual purity and denying the validity of established religions.
1098	Crusaders find a spear in what is now the basement of St. Peter's Cathedral in Acre.
12th c.	The Knights Templar excavate the site of King Solomon's Temple in Jerusalem, allegedly finding several holy relics, possibly including the Ark of the Covenant.

1100	The *Payne Peveril* sections of *Fulk le Fitz Waryn* are written in Medieval Welsh.
1125	Building at Glastonbury hits its peak. William of Malmsbury completes his history of the Abbey called *De Aquitate Glastonie Ecclesie.*
1143–1179	The first *clear* signs of Catharism appear in Cologne, then in Italy.
1184	A great fire at Glastonbury destroys most of the structure, including Joseph's Olde Chirche.
1186	The Lady Chapel consecrated as the site of the Olde Chirche.
1189	Work starts on building the East End of the Great Church.
1190	Chretien writes his Grail text *Le Conte de Graal.*
1191	The tomb allegedly containing the bodies of King Arthur and Guinevere is discovered in the old graveyard immediately to the south of the Lady Chapel.
13th c.	Montreal de S.O.S. is first mentioned.
1200	Robert de Boron writes *Joseph de Arimathie.*
1204	Crusaders take Constantinople, where all the lances had been housed. The conquering knights carry the lances back with them as spoils of war and trophies for Baldwin II.
1213	The Great Church at Glastonbury is consecrated.
1241	Baldwin II sells many relics, including the tip of the original Lance, to King Louis of France. Louis orders the building of the San Chapelle in Paris to house these relics.
1244	The siege of the Cathar stronghold at Montsegur ends with the fall of the castle and the surrender of the Cathars who remained there. Legend states that three Cathar brothers escaped the night before the castle's surrender with the order's most sacred items. Some claim that the Grail was among these sacred objects.
1291	Arthur and Guinevere's bones reburied at the site of the Great Altar at Glastonbury.

13th–14th c.	The Mabinogion is written down, from an oral Tradition, in what is called the Red Book of Hergest.
1350	Charles IV engraves on a golden collar holding the two halves of the spear together the message that this is the true Lance and nails used during Christ's crucifixion.
1492	Pope Innocent VIII reclaims the lance head and shaft from the Turkish Sultan (in return for the Sultan's imprisoned brother), and has the relics hidden in one of the pillars of the high alter in St. John's Basilica. This is also the year that Columbus set sail for his fateful discovery of the West Indies, leading to the discovery of the New World.
1493–1524	St. Joseph's Chapel is created in the "crypt," one level below the Lady Chapel. This is also the year Martin Luther issued his challenge to the Roman Catholic Church.
1534	John Leland states he saw Melkin's book and the passage about Joseph's tomb in the Glastonbury library.
1539	The dissolution of Glastonbury Abbey. The abbey was ransacked and pillaged by Cromwell's forces, and any valuables found were either sold or became part of the King's Treasury.

Bibliography

Begg, Ean, and Deike Begg. *In Search of the Holy Grail and the Precious Blood.* London: Thorsons, 1995.

Boureau, Alain. *The Myth of Pope Joan.* Chicago: University of Chicago Press, 2001.

Cahill, Thomas. *How the Irish Saved Civilization: The Untold Story of Ireland's Heroic Role from the Fall of Rome to the Rise of Medieval Europe.* New York: Doubleday, 1995.

Calvino, Italo. *The Castle of Crossed Destinies.* New York: Harcourt Brace Jovanovich, 1979.

Carley, James P. *Glastonbury Abbey: The Holy House at the Head of the Moors Adventurous.* New York: St. Martin's, 1988.

"The Catholic Encyclopedia." Kevin Knight, copyright 2003, New Advent (www.newadvent.org).

Central Somerset Gazette Official Guide to Glastonbury. Glastonbury: Avalon Press, 1923.

Chrétien de Troyes. *Perceval: or the Story of the Grail.* Translated by Ruth Harwood Cline. Athens: University of Georgia Press, 1985.

Coghlan, Ronan. *The Illustrated Encyclopedia of Arthurian Legends.* New York: Barnes & Noble, 1995.

Drijvers, Jan Willem. *Helena Augusta: The Mother of Constantine the Great and the Legend of Her Finding of the True Cross.* New York: Brill's Studies in Intellectual History, 1992.

Eco, Umberto. *The Name of the Rose.* New York: Harcourt Brace Jovanovich; London: Martin Secker & Warburg, 1983.

Gilbert, Adrian, Alan Wilson, and Baram Blackett. *The Holy Kingdom.* London: Bantam Press, 1998.

Godwin, Malcolm. *The Holy Grail: Its Origins, Secrets and Meaning Revealed.* New York: Viking Studio, 1994.

Goodrich, Norma Lorre. *Merlin*. New York: Harper Perennial, 1988.

The Holy Bible (KJV).

Illustrated Dictionary of Bible Life & Times. New York: Reader's Digest Association, 1989.

The Lais of Marie de France. Translated by Robert W. Hanning and Joan M. Ferrante. Grand Rapids, MI: Baker Book House, 1995.

Lambert, Malcolm. *The Cathars*. Oxford; Malden, MA: Blackwell Publishers, 1998.

Leland, John, ed. *De Rebus Britannicis Collectanea*. 6 vols. London: Gregg International, 1968.

Loomis, Roger Sherman. *The Grail: From Celtic Myth to Christian Symbol*. Princeton, NJ: Princeton University Press, 1991.

The Mabinogion. Translated by Lady Charlotte E. Guest. New York: Dover, 1997.

Matthews, John. *The Elements of the Grail Tradition*. Shaftesbury, England: Element Books, 1990.

The Name of the Rose [film]. 20th Century–Fox, 1986.

The Parzival of Wolfram von Eschenbach. Translated by Edwin H. Zeydel. Studies in the Germanic Languages and Literatures, no. 5. Chapel Hill: University of North Carolina Press, 1951.

Perlesvaus: or the High History of the Holy Grail. Translated by Sebastian Evans. London: J. M. Dent, 1898.

Phillips, Graham. *The Search for the Grail*. London: Century, 1995.

Ravenscroft, Trevor. *The Spear of Destiny*. Maine: Samuel Weiser, 1982.

Rees, B. R. *The Letters of Pelagius and His Followers*. Woodbridge, England; Rochester, NY: Boydell Press, 1991.

Sinclair, Andrew. *The Sword and the Grail: Of the Grail and the Templars and a True Discovery of America*. New York: Crown, 1992.

Staines, David. *The Complete Romances of Chrétien de Troyes*. Bloomington: Indiana University Press, 1990.

Stanford, Peter. *The She-Pope*. London: William Heinemann, 1998.

The Vita Merlini. Studies in Language and Literature, no. 10. Translated by John Jay Parry. Urbana: University of Illinois Press, 1925.

The Voyage of Bran, Son of Febal to the Land of the Living. Translated by Kuno Meyer. 1890.

Waite, Arthur Edward. *The Pictorial Key to the Tarot*. New York: Barnes & Noble, 1995.

Weston, Jessie. *From Ritual to Romance*. New York: Dover, 1997.

Whanger, Mary, and Alan Whanger. *The Shroud of Turin: An Adventure of Discovery*. Tennessee: Providence House Publishers, 1998.

Wilhelm, James J. *The Romance of Arthur: An Anthology of Medieval Texts in Translation*. New York: Garland, 1994.

Zaczek, Iain. *The Chronicles of the Celts*. New York: Sterling, 1996.

Index